UNTETHERED

How to Face Your Wounds, Follow Christ's Truth, and
Rest in God's Peace

RUDOLPH P. VISSER, PHD

Dedication

To **Ena and Ron,**

For we met again, though years had flown,
And in those moments, grace was shown.
Not strangers to pain, nor strangers to grace,
We stood side by side in a sacred place.
A heart that could see where hope still grew—
And named it aloud, when few ever do.
...thank you!

To **the wounded, and those who walk with them**

To the ones shaped by silence and scars,
who carry their stories in hidden places—
May light find you.
May truth name you.
May Christ restore what pain once claimed.

To the hearts that ache beside them,
who choose presence over answers—
May your quiet love speak louder than fear.
May your faith hold space for healing.
May you reflect the mercy of a God who stays.

This journey is long, but not alone.
The Shepherd sees. The Healer moves.
And grace writes the final word.

"He heals the brokenhearted and binds up their wounds."

Psalm 147:3 (ESV)

Contents

Part III
CUTTING THE CORD

Part IV
FLYING FREE

Foreword

In every generation, the Church carries a holy burden: to hold the deep ache of humanity in one hand, and the unshakable promises of God in the other. This book, *Untethered: How to Face Your Wounds, Follow Christ's Truth, and Rest in God's Peace*, enters that sacred space with clarity, courage, and Christ-centered compassion. It speaks into the wounds we carry in our bodies, our memories, our relationships, and even our theology.

Too many believers suffer in silence, unsure how to reconcile their emotional pain with their faith. Some assume true faith should shield them from inner turmoil. Others feel guilt over lingering wounds that won't resolve through Bible verses or Sunday sermons. This book does not dismiss those questions—it dignifies them. It reminds us that healing doesn't come by bypassing pain, but by letting Christ meet us right in the middle of it.

The theological anchor of *Untethered* is unmistakably Reformed. It is rooted in the conviction that God is both sovereign and good—even when our lived experience seems to suggest otherwise. It draws deeply from the well of covenantal theology: God's faithful commitment to His people, and our union with Christ, sustained by the Spirit. Healing here is not self-help—it is sacred participation in God's redeeming work.

What makes this work unique is its integration. The author, Rudolph Visser, draws from trauma-informed psychology, narrative theory, and emotional development, but always filtered through the lens of Scripture. The goal is not to soften theology with therapy, but to show how sound doctrine can actually support true emotional and spiritual restoration. This book is emotionally honest without being indulgent, biblically rich without being rigid, and therapeutically helpful without being clinical.

At its heart, *Untethered* is a journey. It reflects the lived experience of a minister whose pastoral vocation has been shaped over decades—across cities, continents, and contexts. From local congregations to hospital wards, this theology was not only studied, it was lived. Every chapter reflects the voice of someone who has walked with the wounded, sat with the grieving, and witnessed the healing grace of God up close.

To be tethered is to be bound—to false beliefs, to old stories, to identities shaped more by pain than by grace. This book offers more than insight; it offers a path forward. Not by erasing the past, but by letting Christ's voice speak louder than the wounds that have tried to define us.

To every reader who picks up this book with trembling hands or a weary heart: know this—your pain is not too deep, your story is not too complicated, and your healing is not too far off. You are not alone. The Shepherd sees. The Healer moves. And grace, as this book so gently reminds us, writes the final word.

It is with deep joy and gratitude that I commend this work. May it be to you what it has been to me: a companion for the road, a witness to hope, and a call to believe that the gospel is still good news—even for the wounded.

- Rev. Deon Oelofse, MDiv, MTh
Elgin Parish Church, Church of Scotland

Introduction

A Reformed Understanding of Healing

Have you ever watched a helium balloon straining against the string that tethers it to a child's wrist? The balloon seems desperate to soar, to rise into the vast blue sky, yet it remains bound by that nearly invisible string. Many of us live our lives like that balloon—designed to soar, created for freedom, yet mysteriously tethered to something that keeps us earthbound.

These invisible tethers are the painful experiences, traumas, and wounds that have shaped our stories. They're the childhood rejection that whispers "you're not enough," the betrayal that insists "no one can be trusted," or the failure that declares "you'll never succeed." Like nearly invisible strings, these painful narratives direct our movements, limit our choices, and keep us from the freedom God intends for us.

As we begin this journey together, I want to establish an important foundation: God is sovereign over both our suffering and our healing. This isn't a platitude meant to minimize your pain or suggest that God caused your trauma. Rather, it's the bedrock truth that allows us to face our deepest hurts with hope. The Reformed understanding of God's sovereignty doesn't mean God is the author of evil, but it does mean that nothing in our lives—not even our deepest wounds—falls outside His redemptive purposes.

The covenant theology that runs throughout Scripture provides us with a framework for understanding our relationship with God and others. We are not isolated individuals trying to heal ourselves through sheer willpower. We are covenant people, connected to God through Christ and to one another in community. This covenant relationship is the context for our healing journey.

While Scripture is our ultimate authority and guide, God in His common grace has allowed the development of psychological insights that can serve as helpful tools in our healing. Just as we might use antibiotics (a discovery permitted by God's common grace) to treat an infection, we can utilize therapeutic approaches that align with biblical truth to address emotional wounds. The key is evaluating these insights through the lens of Scripture rather than elevating them above God's Word.

The Invisible Tethers: How Pain Shapes Our Lives

Research suggests that approximately 70% of adults have experienced at least one traumatic event in their lifetime, with many experiencing multiple traumas. Even more have endured painful experiences that, while not meeting the clinical definition of trauma, have profoundly shaped their sense of identity and their approach to life.

How do you know if you're living a pain-defined life? Consider these signs:

- You make important life decisions based primarily on avoiding certain feelings or situations
- You have rigid rules for yourself or others that stem from past hurts
- You find yourself repeating destructive patterns in relationships or other areas
- Certain emotional reactions seem disproportionate to current circumstances
- You feel stuck in a narrative about yourself that you know isn't completely true

These patterns reflect the brokenness of our fallen world. Since Adam and Eve's first sin, creation has groaned under the weight of the curse. Our pain doesn't surprise God, nor does it fall outside His sovereign care. As the Psalmist writes, "You have kept count of my tossings; put my tears in your bottle. Are they not in your book?" (Psalm 56:8).

From a Reformed perspective, these pain narratives directly contradict the truth of who we are in Christ and God's sovereign purposes for our lives. When we believe we're "fundamentally broken," we're denying the reality that we are new creations in Christ (2 Corinthians 5:17). When we insist "no one can be trusted," we're forgetting that God is faithful even when humans are not. Our pain narratives often reflect what Reformed theologians call the "noetic effects of sin"—the way sin distorts our thinking and perception.

How Trauma Becomes Identity

When painful experiences occur, especially during childhood or adolescence, they don't just happen to us—they become part of us. Neurologically speaking, traumatic experiences create powerful neural pathways in the brain. These pathways are like well-worn trails through a forest; the more they're traveled, the more established they become, and the more likely we are to automatically follow them in the future.

This is why there's such a profound difference between saying "I experienced trauma" and "I am my trauma." The first statement acknowledges an event that happened to you; the second makes that event the defining feature of your identity. Unfortunately, many of us unconsciously make this shift, allowing our wounds to become the primary lens through which we view ourselves and the world.

Research on identity formation after significant life events shows that we tend to organize our self-concept around emotionally charged experiences, particularly negative ones. This makes evolutionary sense—remembering dangers helps us avoid similar threats in the future. But this survival mechanism can lead us to define ourselves by our worst experiences rather than by the full truth of who we are.

Our tendency toward negative identity formation reflects what Reformed theology understands as total depravity—not that we are as bad as we could possibly be, but that sin affects every aspect of our being, including how we understand ourselves. Apart from God's grace, we naturally gravitate toward distorted self-perception, often defining ourselves by our wounds rather than by God's truth.

The Reformed doctrine of union with Christ offers a powerful counter-narrative. When we come to faith in Christ, we are united with Him in such a profound way that His life, death, and resurrection become ours. As Paul writes in Galatians 2:20, "I have been crucified with Christ. It is no longer I who live, but Christ who lives in me." This means our primary identity is not found in what has happened to us but in who we are in Christ—beloved children of God, chosen before the foundation of the world (Ephesians 1:4).

This doesn't mean we deny or minimize our painful experiences. Rather, it means we refuse to allow those experiences to have the final word about who we are. Our trauma may be part of our story, but in Christ, it's not our defining story.

The Difference Between Remembering and Reliving

One of the most challenging aspects of healing from painful experiences is learning to remember without reliving. When we remember a difficult event, we acknowledge it happened and may feel appropriate emotions about it, but we remain grounded in the present. When we relive a painful experience, we're emotionally transported back to that moment, experiencing the same intensity of feelings, bodily sensations, and thought patterns as during the original event.

Signs you may be reliving rather than remembering include:

- Physical reactions similar to those during the original event (racing heart, shallow breathing, muscle tension)
- Feeling like you're watching a movie of the event rather than simply recalling it
- Losing awareness of your current surroundings

- Experiencing emotions that feel overwhelming or out of proportion
- Finding it difficult to distinguish between past and present threats

Emotional triggering plays a significant role in keeping pain alive. A trigger is anything that reminds you of a traumatic or painful experience—a certain smell, a tone of voice, a particular date on the calendar. When triggered, your brain doesn't always distinguish between past and present danger, activating your fight-flight-freeze response as if the threat were happening now.

Scripture offers profound wisdom for creating distance between ourselves and painful memories. Romans 12:2 instructs us to "be transformed by the renewal of your mind," while 2 Corinthians 10:5 speaks of "taking every thought captive to obey Christ." These verses aren't suggesting we can simply think our way out of trauma, but they do point to the possibility of gaining greater control over our thought patterns with God's help.

Practical techniques for creating this distance include:

- Mindfully observing your thoughts without immediately accepting them as truth
- Using grounding techniques to stay present when memories arise
- Practicing self-compassion rather than judgment when triggered
- Intentionally reminding yourself of what is true now versus what was true then
- Prayerfully inviting God's perspective on painful memories

One of the most powerful steps in healing is simply becoming aware of how past pain has shaped your present life. The following exercise will help you create a visual map of your painful experiences and their ongoing effects. This isn't about dwelling on hurt but about bringing what has been operating in darkness into the light where it can be addressed with God's help.

Begin by finding a quiet space where you won't be interrupted. You'll need several sheets of paper, different colored pens or markers if available, and your Bible. Before starting, take a moment to pray, acknowledging God's sovereignty and presence in your story. You might use words like these:

"Lord, You have known me from before the foundation of the world. Nothing in my story surprises You or falls outside Your sovereign care. As I explore painful parts of my journey, be my guide and comforter. Help me see where I've been defining myself by my wounds rather than by Your truth. Give me courage to face what needs to be faced and wisdom to understand how these experiences have shaped me. In Jesus' name, Amen."

Consider meditating on Psalm 139:1-6, which affirms God's intimate knowledge of every aspect of your life:

"O LORD, you have searched me and known me! You know when I sit down and when I rise up; you discern my thoughts from afar. You search out my path and my lying down and are acquainted with all my ways. Even before a word is on my tongue, behold, O LORD, you know it altogether. You hem me in, behind and before, and lay your hand upon me. Such knowledge is too wonderful for me; it is high; I cannot attain it."

Now, on a large sheet of paper, draw a timeline of your life, marking significant painful experiences. These might include obvious traumas like abuse, accidents, or losses, but also subtler wounds like persistent criticism, emotional neglect, or disappointments. For each event, note:

1. What happened
2. How old you were
3. What conclusion did you draw about yourself, others, or the world
4. How this experience continues to affect you today

Look for patterns across different experiences. Do you notice recurring themes in the conclusions you drew? Are there similarities in how these past events affect your present choices?

On a separate sheet, create a map of your current life. Include major areas such as relationships, work, faith, self-care, and goals. Then, draw lines connecting specific painful experiences from your timeline to the areas of your life they continue to influence. For example, you might link childhood bullying to a current difficulty speaking up in meetings, or a spouse's emotional unavailability to a struggle with intimacy in your marriage.

As you complete this exercise, remember that awareness is the first step toward change. You're not doing this to blame others or to wallow in victimhood, but to understand with compassion how your story has shaped you. This understanding creates space for new choices aligned with your identity in Christ rather than reactions based on past pain.

PART I
THE ROOTS OF OUR STORIES

ONE

The Stories We Carry

"Remember not the former things, nor consider the things of old. Behold, I am doing a new thing; now it springs forth, do you not perceive it?"

Isaiah 43:18-19 (ESV)

In the introduction, we explored the concept of invisible tethers—those painful experiences and narratives that limit our freedom and keep us from soaring into the life God intends for us. We established that God is sovereign over both our suffering and our healing, and that nothing in our lives falls outside His redemptive purposes. Now, we begin the journey of becoming untethered by first acknowledging what binds us: the stories we carry.

Every human being carries stories—narratives about who we are, what the world is like, and how we fit into it. These stories aren't just memories; they're interpretive frameworks that shape how we experience reality. When these stories form around painful experiences, especially those occurring early in life or with significant emotional impact, they can become defining narratives that limit our choices, distort our self-perception, and hinder our spiritual growth.

From a Reformed theological perspective, these limiting narratives reflect what theologians call the "noetic effects of sin"—the way sin distorts our thinking and perception. Our fallen nature inclines us to interpret our experiences in ways that contradict God's truth about who we are and who He is. We naturally gravitate toward self-protective narratives that promise safety but ultimately imprison us in patterns of thinking and behaving that fall short of the freedom Christ secured for us.

The good news is that God's redemptive work includes the renewal of our minds (Romans 12:2). Through His Word and Spirit, God invites us to recognize the stories we've been carrying, examine them in light of His truth, and embrace new narratives aligned with our identity in Christ. This process isn't about denying painful experiences or minimizing their impact. Rather, it's about refusing to allow those experiences to have the final word about who we are and what's possible for our lives.

In this chapter, we'll explore how to identify the pain narratives that may be limiting your life, understand how trauma becomes intertwined with identity, and learn the crucial difference between remembering painful experiences and reliving them. Throughout, we'll ground our understanding in Reformed theological principles while acknowledging the genuine challenge of confronting stories that have shaped us for many years.

Identifying your pain narratives represents the first step in becoming untethered. You can't release what you haven't acknowledged. By bringing these narratives into the light—examining them with compassion rather than judgment—you create space for God's transforming work in your life. As Jesus promised, "You will know the truth, and the truth will set you free" (John 8:32).

Identifying Your Pain Narrative

What is a Pain Narrative?

A pain narrative is a story you've constructed—usually unconsciously—to make sense of painful experiences. It's not just a memory of what happened but an interpretation of what it means about you, others, and the world. These narratives typically form around questions like:

- Why did this happen?
- What does this say about me?
- What does this say about others?
- What does this say about God?
- What must I do to protect myself from similar pain in the future?

For example, a child who experiences persistent criticism might develop a narrative that "I'm fundamentally flawed and must work harder than everyone else to be acceptable." A person who experiences betrayal might conclude, "People can't be trusted with my heart, so I must keep everyone at a safe distance." Someone who prayed fervently for healing that didn't come might decide, "God doesn't really care about my suffering, so I shouldn't expect His help."

These narratives don't form in isolation. They're influenced by:

- The nature and timing of the painful experience
- How others responded to your pain
- Previous experiences and existing beliefs
- Cultural and family messages about suffering
- Theological frameworks for understanding pain

From a Reformed perspective, our pain narratives often reflect what theologians call "common grace insights" mixed with distortions stemming from our fallen nature. The insight that "this experience was genuinely harmful" gets mixed with the distortion that "therefore, I am permanently damaged." The recognition that "this person hurt me intentionally" becomes entangled with the generalization that "therefore, no one can be trusted." These distortions aren't just psychological errors but spiritual ones—they contradict God's truth about who He is, who we are in Christ, and His redemptive purposes for our lives.

Common Pain Narratives

While each person's story is unique, certain pain narratives appear consistently across different experiences and backgrounds. These include:

The Defectiveness Narrative: "There's something fundamentally wrong with me that makes me unworthy of love and belonging."

This narrative often forms in childhood through experiences of persistent criticism, emotional neglect, or comparison to siblings or peers. It creates a sense of shame that goes beyond feeling bad about actions to feeling bad about one's very being. People carrying this narrative typically engage in perfectionism, people-pleasing, or self-sabotage, either trying to compensate for perceived defectiveness or acting in ways that confirm it.

From a Reformed perspective, the defectiveness narrative contradicts the truth that while we are indeed fallen and sinful, we are also created in God's image (Genesis 1:27) and, if believers, have been made new creations in Christ (2 Corinthians 5:17). It confuses the Reformed doctrine of total depravity (the pervasiveness of sin's effects) with a false notion that we are worthless or beyond redemption.

The Abandonment Narrative: "People always leave. I'll never be someone's priority."

This narrative typically forms through experiences of significant loss, rejection, or inconsistent care. It creates hypervigilance about others' commitment and availability, often leading to clingy behavior that ironically pushes others away or preemptive rejection to avoid the pain of being left. People carrying this narrative may test relationships repeatedly or avoid deep connection altogether.

From a Reformed perspective, the abandonment narrative contradicts the truth of God's covenant faithfulness and the security we have in Christ. While human relationships may indeed disappoint us, "neither death nor life, nor angels nor rulers, nor things present nor things to come, nor powers, nor height nor depth, nor anything else in all creation, will be able to separate us from the love of God in Christ Jesus our Lord" (Romans 8:38-39).

The Powerlessness Narrative: "I have no control over what happens to me. I'm at the mercy of circumstances and others' choices."

This narrative typically forms through experiences where one's agency was violated or where attempts to change painful circumstances repeatedly failed. It creates a sense of learned helplessness, where people stop trying to influence their circumstances even when opportunities for change exist. People carrying this narrative often engage in passive behavior, excessive compliance, or self-destructive choices that confirm their lack of agency.

From a Reformed perspective, the powerlessness narrative reflects a distortion of the doctrine of God's sovereignty. While Reformed theology emphasizes God's control over all things, it also affirms human responsibility and the genuine agency we exercise as image-bearers. We are not passive objects but active participants in God's redemptive work, "for it is God who works in you, both to will and to work for his good pleasure" (Philippians 2:13).

The Betrayal Narrative: "People can't be trusted. If I let my guard down, I'll be hurt again."

This narrative typically forms through experiences of significant betrayal, deception, or exploitation, particularly by those in positions of trust. It creates hypervigilance about others' motives and trustworthiness, often leading to controlling behavior, suspicion, or isolation. People carrying this narrative may test others repeatedly or maintain superficial connections while avoiding genuine vulnerability.

From a Reformed perspective, the betrayal narrative reflects the reality of human sinfulness but fails to account for common grace —the way God restrains evil and enables genuine goodness even in those who don't know Him. While wisdom includes appropriate discernment about others' trustworthiness, the betrayal narrative contradicts the biblical call to love, which "bears all things, believes all things, hopes all things, endures all things" (1 Corinthians 13:7).

The Insignificance Narrative: "Nothing I do matters. My life has no meaningful impact."

This narrative typically forms through experiences where one's contributions were consistently ignored, dismissed, or criticized. It creates a sense of futility about one's efforts and gifts, often leading to underachievement, lack of direction, or desperate attempts to prove one's worth through achievement. People carrying this narrative may avoid setting goals, sabotage success, or become workaholics trying to establish their value.

From a Reformed perspective, the insignificance narrative contradicts the truth that God works all things according to His purpose (Ephesians 1:11) and that even our smallest actions can have eternal significance when done for His glory (Colossians 3:23-24). It fails to recognize that our primary purpose isn't found in visible impact but in faithful obedience to our calling as image-bearers.

Identifying Your Personal Pain Narrative

Recognizing your own pain narratives require honest self-reflection and a willingness to examine patterns in your thinking, feeling, and behaving. Consider the following questions:

1. What painful experiences have had the most significant impact on your life?
2. What conclusions did you draw about yourself, others, God, or the world from these experiences?
3. What rules do you live by to protect yourself from similar pain?

4. What patterns do you notice in your relationships, work, faith, or self-care?

5. What do you find yourself saying to yourself when you're most distressed?

For example, you might notice that you consistently choose romantic partners who need "fixing," work jobs below your capability, avoid close friendships, or maintain rigid control over your environment. These patterns often point to underlying narratives formed through painful experiences.

As you identify these narratives, approach them with compassion rather than judgment. Remember that these stories didn't form because you were weak or foolish but because you were trying to make sense of painful experiences with the resources available to you at the time. They represent your mind's attempt to protect you from further harm, even if they now limit your freedom and contradict what you consciously believe to be true.

From a Reformed perspective, identifying your pain narratives isn't just psychological work but spiritual discernment. It involves recognizing how sin—both others' sin against you and the noetic effects of sin on your own thinking—has shaped your understanding of yourself and God. This discernment creates space for the Spirit's transforming work as you bring these narratives into the light of God's truth.

How Trauma Becomes Identity

The Neurological Impact of Trauma

To understand how painful experiences become intertwined with identity, it helps to understand what happens in the brain during and after traumatic events. When we experience something threatening or overwhelming, our brain's alarm system—centered in the amygdala—activates our fight-flight-freeze response. This survival mechanism bypasses our rational thinking centers to enable immediate protective action.

In normal circumstances, once the threat passes, our nervous system returns to baseline, and the experience gets processed into narrative memory—the kind we can recall and tell as a story with a beginning, middle, and end. But when experiences are particularly overwhelming or occur during developmentally vulnerable periods, they may not get processed normally. Instead, they remain stored as implicit, fragmented memories that continue to trigger our alarm system when activated by reminders of the original event.

This neurological impact helps explain why traumatic experiences feel different from ordinary difficult memories. They don't just influence what we think about ourselves but how we experience ourselves at a bodily level. When triggered, we don't just remember feeling afraid or ashamed—we re-experience those emotions with the same intensity as during the original event. This immediate, embodied quality makes trauma-based identity particularly powerful and resistant to change through rational insight alone.

From a Reformed perspective, this neurological understanding reflects the biblical truth that we are embodied souls, not just thinking minds. Our physical brain structure and functioning are part of how God designed us as image-bearers, and the way trauma impacts these systems reflects the comprehensive effects of the Fall on every aspect of human functioning. Understanding these neurological mechanisms doesn't diminish spiritual realities but helps us appreciate the complexity of God's design and the multifaceted nature of healing.

From Event to Identity

The shift from "I experienced trauma" to "I am my trauma" typically happens through several interrelated processes:

Meaning-making. Humans naturally seek to make meaning of their experiences, particularly painful ones. When trauma occurs, especially in childhood before we have mature cognitive frameworks, we often make meaning in ways that place responsibility on ourselves rather than acknowledging our vulnerability in situations beyond our control. A child who experiences abuse might conclude "I'm bad" rather than recognizing "I was harmed by someone who should have protected me." These meaning structures become incorporated into our fundamental understanding of who we are.

Emotional conditioning. Through repeated experiences or single overwhelming events, certain emotions become strongly associated with our sense of self. If shame, fear, or worthlessness were prominent during traumatic experiences, these emotions may become our baseline state—how we automatically feel about ourselves unless actively thinking otherwise. This emotional conditioning operates largely outside conscious awareness, creating a felt sense of identity that may contradict what we intellectually believe about ourselves.

Protective adaptations. To survive painful experiences, we develop adaptations that help us cope—hypervigilance, emotional numbing, people-pleasing, perfectionism, or various forms of self-protection. Over time, these adaptations become so familiar that we mistake them for our personality rather than recognizing them as strategies developed in response to specific threats. We might think "I'm just a private person" rather than recognizing "I learned to hide my true self because vulnerability wasn't safe."

Narrative reinforcement. Once formed, trauma-based identity gets reinforced through the stories we tell ourselves and others. We selectively attend to experiences that confirm our narrative while minimizing or reinterpreting contradictory evidence. If we believe "I'm fundamentally unlovable," we'll notice every instance of rejection while discounting genuine expressions of care. This selective attention creates a self-reinforcing cycle that maintains trauma-based identity even in the face of new, potentially healing experiences.

Social mirroring. Our sense of identity is also shaped by how others see and treat us. If painful experiences lead others to label us or interact with us based on our trauma (e.g., treating an abuse survivor as perpetually fragile), this social mirroring can reinforce a trauma-based identity. Conversely, being seen and treated according to our true identity in Christ by a supportive community can powerfully counteract trauma-based narratives.

From a Reformed perspective, the process by which trauma becomes identity highlights the pervasive effects of sin on both individual psychology and social dynamics. It also underscores the importance of the church community as a context where believers can experience being known and loved according to their identity in Christ rather than their painful pasts. As the Heidelberg Catechism affirms, belonging to Christ means "I am not my own, but belong—body and soul, in life and in death—to my faithful Savior, Jesus Christ" (HC Q.1). This fundamental belonging provides the secure foundation from which we can challenge trauma-based identities.

The Difference Between Remembering and Reliving

Understanding Triggers

As mentioned in the introduction, a crucial distinction in healing is learning to remember painful experiences without reliving them. Reliving often happens through emotional triggers—sensory inputs or situations that remind our brain of past trauma and activate the fight-flight-freeze response as if the threat were happening now.

Triggers can be:

- **External:** People, places, sights, sounds, smells, tastes, or specific dates associated with the painful experience.
- **Internal:** Thoughts, feelings, bodily sensations, or memories that arise spontaneously.

Understanding your personal triggers is essential for managing them effectively. Pay attention to situations or internal states that seem to evoke disproportionately strong emotional reactions. Keep a log if helpful:

- What happened just before the strong reaction?
- What were you thinking, feeling, and sensing in your body?
- Did the situation remind you of anything from your past?

Recognizing triggers doesn't mean avoiding them entirely—that often leads to a shrinking life. Instead, it means developing strategies for responding differently when triggered, reminding yourself that the current situation is not the past danger.

From a Reformed perspective, understanding triggers helps us appreciate the ongoing effects of living in a fallen world while affirming the power of God's grace to enable new responses. We acknowledge the reality of our embodied experience—how past events continue to affect our nervous system—while trusting that the Spirit empowers us to "walk by the Spirit, and you will not gratify the desires of the flesh" (Galatians 5:16), including bodily reactions rooted in past trauma.

Grounding Techniques

Grounding techniques are practical tools for staying present when painful memories or triggers arise, helping you remember without reliving. They work by redirecting your attention to your current sensory experience, reminding your brain that you are safe in the present moment.

Examples of grounding techniques include:

- **5-4-3-2-1 Sensory Awareness:** Name five things you can see, four things you can touch, three things you can hear, two things you can smell, and one thing you can taste.

- **Physical Grounding:** Press your feet firmly into the floor, notice the sensation of the chair supporting you, or hold onto a textured object.
- **Mental Grounding:** Describe your surroundings in detail, count backward from 100 by sevens, or name all the objects you see of a certain color.
- **Self-Soothing:** Use comforting sensory input like listening to calming music, smelling essential oils, wrapping yourself in a blanket, or drinking warm tea.

Experiment to find which techniques work best for you. Practice them when you're calm so they become familiar and accessible when needed.

From a Reformed perspective, grounding techniques can be seen as practical applications of biblical principles like mindfulness (being aware of the present moment without judgment) and stewardship of our bodies (recognizing our physical experience as part of God's creation). They don't replace spiritual disciplines but can complement them by helping regulate our nervous system so we can engage more fully with God's truth and presence.

Creating Distance Through Observation

Another strategy for remembering without reliving involves creating psychological distance by observing your thoughts and feelings without immediately identifying with them. This is sometimes called "mindful observation" or "cognitive defusion."

Instead of thinking "I am anxious," try reframing it as "I am noticing the feeling of anxiety." Instead of "This thought is true," try "I am having the thought that..."

This subtle shift in language creates space between you (the observer) and your internal experience (the thoughts and feelings). It allows you to acknowledge what you're experiencing without being overwhelmed or defined by it. You can recognize a painful memory or a triggered emotion as something happening within you rather than something that constitutes the entirety of you.

From a Reformed perspective, this practice aligns with the biblical call to self-examination (2 Corinthians 13:5) and discernment (Philippians 1:9-10). It involves bringing our internal world before God, asking for His perspective, and evaluating our thoughts and feelings against the standard of His Word. We don't simply accept our internal experience as authoritative but submit it to God's truth.

As we conclude this chapter, remember that identifying your pain narratives and understanding how they became intertwined with your identity is a significant step toward freedom. This awareness creates the foundation for the work we'll explore in subsequent chapters: challenging these narratives, processing the underlying emotions, and embracing new stories grounded in God's redemptive purposes. The journey may feel daunting, but you don't walk it alone. God, who began a good work in you, **will be faithful to complete it (Philippians 1:6).**

TWO

The Cost Of Staying Tethered

"For freedom Christ has set us free; stand firm therefore, and do not submit again to a yoke of slavery."

Galatians 5:1 (ESV)

I n the previous chapter, we explored how to identify the pain narratives that may be limiting your life. We examined how trauma becomes intertwined with identity and learned the crucial difference between remembering painful experiences and reliving them. Now, we turn to an honest assessment of what these pain narratives cost us when we remain tethered to them.

Many of us have lived with our pain for so long that we've normalized its presence. Like someone who has grown accustomed to chronic physical pain, we may no longer recognize how much energy we expend accommodating our emotional wounds. We've adapted to their limitations, perhaps even building our identities around them, until the very thought of living differently seems not just frightening but almost impossible to imagine.

From a Reformed theological perspective, this accommodation reflects what Scripture calls "conforming to the pattern of this world" (Romans 12:2). We've accepted a diminished version of life as normal rather than embracing the "abundant life" Jesus promises (John 10:10). Our pain narratives have become familiar companions, and like the Israelites who sometimes longed for the familiarity of Egyptian slavery over the uncertainties of freedom, we may unconsciously cling to our limitations rather than stepping into the spacious place God intends for us.

In this chapter, we'll explore the very real costs of staying tethered to our pain. We'll examine how these invisible restraints limit our choices, affect our physical health, shape our relationships, and ultimately keep us from the abundant life God intends for us. By honestly assessing what our pain is costing us, we create motivation for the challenging but rewarding work of breaking free.

Recognizing Patterns of Self-Limitation

The Invisible Fences We Create

Most of us don't consciously decide to limit our lives. Instead, we develop subtle patterns of self-protection that, over time, become so habitual we no longer notice them. These "safety behaviors" might have been necessary or helpful when we first experienced pain, but they eventually become prisons that keep us from growth and fulfillment.

Common self-limiting patterns include:

- **Avoidance:** Steering clear of situations, people, or emotions that might trigger painful feelings
- **Perfectionism:** Attempting to control outcomes through flawless performance
- **People-pleasing:** Sacrificing authenticity to maintain others' approval
- **Procrastination:** Delaying action to avoid potential failure or disappointment
- **Numbing:** Using substances, technology, busyness, or other distractions to avoid feeling
- **Hypervigilance:** Remaining constantly on alert for potential threats
- **Self-sabotage:** Unconsciously undermining success when it approaches

From a Reformed perspective, these patterns often reflect a fundamental lack of trust in God's sovereignty and goodness. When we avoid risk because we fear failure, we're essentially saying we don't trust God to work all things for good as He promises in Romans 8:28. When we people-please to avoid rejection, we're placing others' opinions above God's unchanging love for us. Our self-limiting behaviors, while understandable, often reveal places where our theology hasn't fully transformed our practical living.

Scripture directly addresses this tension in Proverbs 3:5-6: "Trust in the LORD with all your heart, and do not lean on your own understanding. In all your ways acknowledge him, and he will make straight your paths." Our self-protective patterns often represent leaning on our own understanding rather than trusting God's sovereign guidance.

As theologian Herman Bavinck writes in his *Reformed Dogmatics*, "Faith is not only a certain knowledge by which I accept as true all that God has revealed to us in his Word, but also a wholehearted trust which the Holy Spirit works in me through the gospel" (Bavinck, 2008, p. 83). Our self-limiting patterns often reveal where wholehearted trust remains challenging.

The Reformed concept of "total inability"—our complete dependence on God's grace for spiritual transformation—reminds us that breaking these patterns isn't simply a matter of trying harder. We need the Holy Spirit's work to renew our minds and hearts, enabling us to trust God's purposes even when the path forward seems uncertain or frightening.

The Reinforcement Cycle

What makes these patterns so persistent is how they reinforce themselves. When we avoid a situation that causes anxiety, we experience immediate relief—a powerful reward that strengthens the avoidance behavior. However, we never get the opportunity to discover that we might have handled the situation successfully, so our fear remains unchallenged.

Neurologically speaking, avoidance creates a reinforcement cycle. Each time we avoid something frightening, our brain registers a "success"—we escaped the perceived threat. This strengthens the neural pathway connecting that situation with danger and avoidance with safety. Over time, these pathways become so established that our avoidance feels automatic and necessary rather than chosen.

This creates a painful paradox: the very behaviors that protect us in the short-term harm us in the long-term. As psychologist

Judith Herman notes in her landmark work *Trauma and Recovery*, "The conflict between the will to deny horrible events and the will to proclaim them aloud is the central dialectic of psychological trauma" (Herman, 2015, p. 1). We simultaneously need both safety and freedom, yet our protective mechanisms often prevent the very growth that would ultimately make us safer.

From a Reformed perspective, this tension reflects the "already but not yet" nature of our sanctification. We are already new creations in Christ (2 Corinthians 5:17), yet we await the completion of our transformation. Growth requires courage to step beyond established patterns, trusting God's presence even in discomfort.

For example, consider how avoidance reinforces itself. A talented writer might avoid sharing her work due to childhood criticism that left her feeling inadequate. Each time she considers submitting an article or joining a writing group, anxiety arises. By choosing not to share her writing, the anxiety immediately subsides—reinforcing the avoidance. Yet she never discovers that her work might be well-received, or that she could handle criticism without being devastated. The very behavior that provides short-term relief ensures long-term limitation.

This perspective helps us recognize that our avoidance isn't just about protecting ourselves from criticism; it reflects a deeper lack of trust in God's purposes for our lives and work. If God has given us gifts, who are we to hide them? This realization doesn't immediately dissolve fear, but it does provide a theological framework for challenging it. With support from a church community, we can begin taking small steps toward sharing our work, gradually expanding beyond the invisible fence that has contained us for so long.

Identifying Your Patterns

Take a moment to reflect on your own life. Where might you be living within invisible fences created by past pain? Consider these questions:

- What opportunities or experiences do you consistently avoid?
- Are there areas of life where you hold back or play small?
- What would you do differently if you knew you couldn't fail?
- Where do you find yourself saying "I can't" or "That's not for people like me"?
- What dreams have you set aside because they feel too risky?

As you identify these patterns, try to connect them to their origins. When did you first learn to limit yourself in this way? What experience taught you this boundary was necessary? And most importantly, how might these limitations reflect places where trust in God's sovereignty remains difficult?

The Physical Toll of Emotional Baggage

The Body Keeps the Score

We often think of emotional pain as purely psychological, but our bodies tell a different story. Research increasingly confirms what many have intuitively known: emotional wounds manifest physically. As psychiatrist Bessel van der Kolk writes in his influential book *The Body Keeps the Score*, "The body continues to defend against a threat that belongs to the past" (van der Kolk, 2014, p. 45).

Common physical manifestations of unprocessed emotional pain include:

- Chronic tension in specific muscle groups
- Digestive issues and inflammation
- Sleep disturbances
- Compromised immune function
- Chronic fatigue
- Unexplained pain
- Shallow breathing patterns
- Heightened startle response

These physical symptoms aren't imaginary or "all in your head"— they're real physiological responses to emotional distress. Your body doesn't distinguish between physical and emotional threats; both activate the same stress response systems.

From a Reformed perspective, this mind-body connection reflects our creation as unified beings. Unlike some philosophical traditions that separate the spiritual from the physical, Reformed theology has historically emphasized the wholeness of human personhood. As theologian Anthony Hoekema writes in *Created in God's Image*, "The Bible does not teach a body-soul dualism in which the soul is considered the essential person and the body a kind of prison from which the soul will ultimately be liberated" (Hoekema, 1994, p. 203).

This holistic understanding means we cannot separate spiritual healing from physical wellbeing. When Scripture speaks of the body as the temple of the Holy Spirit (1 Corinthians 6:19-20), it affirms the sacredness of our physical existence and the importance of caring for our bodies as part of our spiritual discipleship.

The Reformed understanding of the resurrection body also provides hope in the midst of physical suffering. As Paul writes in Romans 8:23, "we ourselves, who have the firstfruits of the Spirit, groan inwardly as we wait eagerly for adoption as sons, the redemption of our bodies." Our current physical suffering is not the end of the story; we await bodies that will be fully redeemed and restored, free from the effects of sin and pain.

Allostatic Load and Chronic Stress

When we carry unresolved emotional pain, our bodies often remain in a state of low-grade emergency. Scientists call the cumulative wear and tear of chronic stress "allostatic load." Like a car constantly running in high gear, our bodies weren't designed to sustain emergency responses indefinitely.

Over time, this persistent stress response can lead to serious health consequences, including:

- Cardiovascular problems
- Hormonal imbalances
- Accelerated aging
- Increased vulnerability to illness
- Cognitive impairment
- Metabolic issues

These effects reflect what Reformed theology understands as the comprehensive impact of the fall on human existence. Sin's effects extend to every aspect of creation, including our physical bodies. As theologian Michael Horton notes in *The Christian Faith*, "In contrast to Greek thought, biblical faith does not locate sin in the physical body but in the heart... Nevertheless, our physical condition bears the marks of our fallenness" (Horton, 2011, p. 423).

This theological perspective helps us understand our physical symptoms not as punishment but as manifestations of living in a fallen world where sin's effects touch every dimension of our being. It also points us toward the hope of comprehensive redemption that includes our bodies (Romans 8:23).

For example, consider how chronic stress affects the body. A man who experienced childhood neglect might carry a constant sense of hypervigilance—always scanning for potential rejection or abandonment. This persistent state of alertness keeps stress hormones elevated, eventually contributing to high blood pressure, disrupted sleep, and digestive problems. Though he might attribute these issues solely to genetics or lifestyle, they're partly manifestations of carrying unresolved emotional pain.

Understanding this connection doesn't mean these physical symptoms are "just psychological." Rather, it acknowledges the profound interconnection between our emotional, spiritual, and physical dimensions—a holistic view consistent with biblical anthropology.

Body Awareness Exercise

Our bodies often recognize what our minds deny. Learning to listen to your body's signals can provide important information about your emotional state and unresolved pain. Try this simple practice:

1. Find a quiet place where you won't be disturbed. Sit comfortably with your feet on the floor and your hands resting in your lap.
2. Take several deep breaths, allowing your attention to settle into your body.
3. Slowly scan from the top of your head to your feet, noticing any areas of tension, discomfort, or other sensations.
4. When you identify a sensation, approach it with curiosity rather than judgment. Ask: What is this sensation trying to tell me? Is there an emotion connected to this physical feeling?
5. Notice if certain thoughts or memories arise as you attend to different areas of your body.
6. Close by thanking God for the wisdom of your body and asking for guidance in addressing what you've discovered.

This practice aligns with the biblical invitation to present our bodies as living sacrifices (Romans 12:1) and to acknowledge God's intimate knowledge of our physical being (Psalm 139:13-14). By attending to our bodies with compassionate awareness, we honor God's design and gain valuable insights for our healing journey.

Relationships Shaped by Past Pain

The Projection Pattern

One of the most significant costs of unhealed pain is its impact on our relationships. We don't experience people as they actually are, but through the lens of our past hurts and expectations. Psychologists call this "projection"—we project our pain narratives onto current relationships, often recreating the very dynamics we fear.

For example, someone who was abandoned as a child might be hypervigilant about any signs of potential abandonment in adult relationships. They might interpret a partner's need for alone time as rejection, or a friend's busy schedule as disinterest. These interpretations then trigger protective behaviors—perhaps becoming clingy or preemptively pulling away—creating the very abandonment they fear.

This tendency reflects what Reformed theology understands as the noetic effects of sin—the way sin distorts our perception and thinking. As theologian Cornelius Van Til observed, sin affects not just our moral choices but our entire cognitive framework. Our pain narratives become interpretive grids through which we filter all relational data, often in ways that reinforce our existing beliefs rather than accurately perceiving reality.

Scripture acknowledges this tendency when it warns against judging others (Matthew 7:1-5), noting how our own "logs" affect our perception of others' "specks." Our unhealed wounds become these logs, distorting our vision and preventing us from seeing others clearly.

This distortion often extends to how we perceive the image of God in others. Genesis 1:27 tells us that all humans are created in God's image, yet our pain can blind us to this reality, causing us to see others primarily as potential sources of threat or disappointment rather than bearers of divine image. Healing our perception allows us to more clearly recognize and honor God's image in those around us.

Attraction to the Familiar

Another costly relationship pattern is our tendency to be drawn to what's familiar, even when it's harmful. Many people find themselves repeatedly attracted to partners who trigger their core wounds or recreate childhood dynamics. This isn't because they consciously want to be hurt, but because these patterns feel familiar and predictable, even if painful.

Psychologists sometimes call this "repetition compulsion"—an unconscious drive to repeat past traumas in an attempt to master them. However, without conscious awareness and intentional change, these repetitions usually just reinforce the original wounds.

From a Reformed perspective, this pattern reflects the bondage of sin described in Romans 7:15: "For I do not understand my own actions. For I do not do what I want, but I do the very thing I hate." Our fallen nature inclines us toward patterns that ultimately harm us, even when we consciously desire something different. Recognizing this tendency helps us approach our relationship patterns with humility and dependence on God's grace for transformation.

It also highlights the importance of Christian community in providing alternative models of relationship. As we experience healthy, Christ-centered relationships within the church, we develop new templates for intimacy that can counteract the pull toward familiar but harmful patterns.

The Impact on Intimacy

Unhealed pain creates significant barriers to genuine intimacy. Vulnerability feels too risky, trust seems impossible, and emotional closeness triggers fears of being overwhelmed or abandoned. Common intimacy challenges include:

- **Fear of engulfment:** Worrying that closeness will lead to losing oneself
- **Fear of abandonment:** Believing that intimacy inevitably leads to rejection
- **Difficulty with vulnerability:** Hiding true thoughts and feelings to avoid judgment
- **Controlling behavior:** Attempting to manage relationships to prevent hurt
- **Emotional unavailability:** Keeping others at a distance to maintain safety

These challenges reflect a fundamental misunderstanding of biblical intimacy, which involves both vulnerability and healthy boundaries. True intimacy, modeled in God's covenant relationship with His people, requires trust, honesty, and mutual self-giving—qualities often undermined by past pain.

From a Reformed perspective, our capacity for intimacy is rooted in our creation as relational beings made in the image of a triune God. Sin has damaged this capacity, but Christ's redemptive work restores it. As we grow in our understanding of God's unconditional love for us in Christ, we find the security needed to risk vulnerability in human relationships.

The Spiritual Cost

Distorted View of God

Perhaps the most profound cost of staying tethered to our pain is how it distorts our view of God. Our experiences, particularly painful ones involving authority figures or unmet needs, often become the lens through which we interpret God's character and actions.

- Someone wounded by a critical parent might perceive God primarily as a harsh judge.
- Someone abandoned by a caregiver might struggle to trust God's faithfulness.
- Someone whose prayers for healing went unanswered might view God as distant or uncaring.

These distortions reflect what Reformed theology calls idolatry—allowing something other than God's self-revelation in Scripture to define our understanding of Him. As John Calvin writes in his *Institutes*, "Man's nature, so to speak, is a perpetual factory of idols" (Calvin, 1559/2008, 1.11.8). Our painful experiences can become these idols, shaping our perception of God in ways that contradict His revealed character.

This distorted view prevents us from experiencing the fullness of our relationship with God. We might approach Him with fear rather than confidence, doubt His love even while intellectually affirming it, or keep Him at arm's length to avoid potential disappointment. Healing involves recognizing these distortions and intentionally replacing them with a biblically grounded understanding of God's character—His sovereignty, wisdom, goodness, faithfulness, and love revealed most fully in Christ.

Hindered Spiritual Growth

Unresolved pain also hinders our spiritual growth. When significant emotional energy is tied up managing past wounds, less is available for pursuing spiritual disciplines, serving others, or engaging fully in community.

Common spiritual hindrances include:

- Difficulty trusting God's promises
- Struggling with prayer or Bible reading due to emotional triggers
- Avoiding vulnerability in Christian community
- Feeling unworthy of God's grace or forgiveness
- Interpreting present difficulties as punishment for past sins

These hindrances reflect the ongoing battle between the flesh and the Spirit described in Galatians 5. Our unhealed wounds become strongholds of the flesh, resisting the Spirit's transforming work. Addressing these wounds isn't separate from spiritual growth but an integral part of it—clearing the ground so the Spirit can produce His fruit more fully in our lives.

From a Reformed perspective, this process aligns with the doctrine of sanctification—the ongoing work of the Spirit conforming us to the image of Christ. As the Westminster Shorter Catechism states, sanctification involves being "enabled more and more to die unto sin, and live unto righteousness" (WSC Q.35).

Dying unto sin includes addressing the ways past pain continues to shape our present thoughts, feelings, and behaviors.

Missing Out on Abundant Life

Ultimately, staying tethered to our pain keeps us from experiencing the abundant life Jesus promises (John 10:10). This abundant life isn't necessarily free from difficulty but characterized by freedom, joy, purpose, and deep connection with God and others —qualities often obscured by the weight of unhealed wounds.

When we live tethered, we operate from a place of deficit— focused on avoiding pain rather than pursuing God's purposes. We make choices based on fear rather than faith, limit our potential based on past failures, and relate to others through the lens of past hurts. This isn't the freedom for which Christ set us free (Galatians 5:1).

Breaking free requires courage to face the cost of staying tethered and faith to believe that a different way of living is possible through Christ. It involves acknowledging the limitations we've accepted and choosing to pursue the fullness of life God offers, even when it feels unfamiliar or frightening.

As we conclude this chapter, take time to honestly assess what staying tethered is costing you. What limitations have you accepted? What physical symptoms might be connected to emotional pain? How are your relationships affected? How is your view of God distorted? Acknowledging these costs provides the motivation needed for the journey ahead—the journey toward becoming untethered and embracing the freedom found in Christ.

Worksheet 1: Mapping Your Pain

Instructions: Reflect on the areas in your life where you feel "tethered" or experience recurring pain *(emotional, relational, spiritual, or even physical pain linked to emotional states)*. Use the space below to map these out. Consider the source, the feeling, and the situations where this pain typically arises. This exercise is about honest acknowledgment, not judgment.

Area of Pain 1:

- **Description:**

_____

_____

(What is the pain? e.g., Fear of rejection, chronic self-doubt, unresolved anger)

- **Source** (if known):

_____

_____

(Where do you think this originates? e.g., Past experiences, specific relationships, internal beliefs)

- **Feelings Associated:**

_____

_____

(List the primary emotions: e.g., Sadness, anxiety, frustration, shame)

- **Trigger Situations:**

_____

_____

(When does this pain usually surface? e.g., Social gatherings, performance reviews, family interactions)

Area of Pain 2:

- **Description:**

_____

_____

- **Source (if known):**

_____

_____

- **Feelings Associated:**

_____

_____

- **Trigger Situations:**

_____

_____

Area of Pain 3:

- **Description:**

_____

_____

- **Source (if known):**

_____

_____

- **Feelings Associated:**

_____

_____

- **Trigger Situations:**

_____

_____

Reflection:

- Looking at your map, do you notice any patterns or connections between these areas of pain?

_____

_____

- How does acknowledging these tethers feel?

_____

_____

- "The Lord is near to the brokenhearted and saves the crushed in spirit" (Psalm 34:18). How does this verse speak to you as you look at your pain map?

_____

_____

Worksheet 2: Identifying Your Narratives

Instructions: Reflect on the core narratives or stories you tell yourself about your pain, your identity, or your circumstances, as discussed in Chapter 1. What recurring themes or beliefs shape your understanding of your experiences? Use the prompts below to identify and examine one significant narrative.

a. **Narrative Identified:**

_____

_____

(Briefly describe the story you tell yourself, e.g., "I'm not good enough," "I'll always be stuck in this situation," "My past defines me.")

b. **Where did this narrative come from?**

_____

_____

(Consider past experiences, messages received from others, interpretations of events.)

c. **How does this narrative make you feel?**

_____

_____

(List associated emotions: e.g., Hopelessness, inadequacy, resentment, fear.)

d. **How does this narrative influence your thoughts, feelings, and actions?**

_____

_____

(Provide specific examples.)

Challenging the Narrative with Truth:

- **Is this narrative 100% true all the time?** (Look for exceptions or counter-evidence.)
- **What biblical truths contradict or offer a different perspective on this narrative?**

(Recall relevant scripture or theological concepts, e.g., Identity in Christ, God's sovereignty, promise of redemption.)

Scripture/Concept 1:

_____

How it applies:

_____

Scripture/Concept 2:

_____

How it applies:

_____

Prayer: Ask God to help you see this narrative through His eyes and to replace lies with His truth. "And you will know the truth, and the truth will set you free" (John 8:32).

Worksheet 3: Body Scan Awareness

Instructions: Find a quiet place where you can sit comfortably without distractions for 5-10 minutes. Gently close your eyes or soften your gaze. Bring your attention inward, focusing on the physical sensations in your body. This exercise, adapted from Chapter 2, helps connect emotional states to physical feelings.

Preparation: Take a few slow, deep breaths. Settle into your chair.

Scan:

1. **Feet and Legs:** Bring your awareness to your feet. Notice any sensations – warmth, coolness, tingling, pressure, tightness, relaxation. Slowly move your attention up through your ankles, calves, knees, and thighs. Just observe without judgment.
   - *Sensations Noticed:*

   _____

   _____

2. **Hips and Torso:** Shift your focus to your hips, lower back, abdomen, and chest. Are there areas of tension, openness, warmth, or discomfort? Notice the gentle rise and fall of your breath in your belly or chest.
   - *Sensations Noticed:*

   _____

   _____

3. **Arms and Hands:** Bring your awareness to your shoulders, down your arms, to your elbows, forearms, wrists, and hands. Notice any sensations present.
   - *Sensations Noticed:*

   _____

   _____

4. **Neck and Head:** Gently scan your neck, throat, jaw, face, and scalp. Are you holding tension anywhere? Notice the temperature of the air on your skin.
   - *Sensations Noticed:*

   _____

   _____

Reflection:

- Were you surprised by any sensations you noticed?

_____

_____

- Did you notice any connection between a physical sensation and a current emotion or thought?

_____

_____

- How did it feel to simply observe your body without trying to change anything?

_____

_____

"Do you not know that your bodies are temples of the Holy Spirit, who is in you, whom you have received from God? You are not your own; you were bought at a price. Therefore honor God with your bodies"

1 Corinthians 6:19-20

How does paying gentle, non-judgmental attention to your body align with honoring God with it?

_____

_____

THREE

Why We Hold On

> *"The heart is deceitful above all things, and desperately sick; who can understand it?"*
>
> Jeremiah 17:9 (ESV)

Have you ever found yourself holding onto something broken? Perhaps it was a chipped mug that somehow meant more to you than the pristine ones in your cabinet. Or maybe it was a tattered sweater with holes at the elbows that you couldn't bear to discard. We all have these objects—items that have outlived their practical usefulness but retain a powerful emotional hold on us.

In many ways, our pain functions like these treasured broken objects. Even when we clearly see what it costs us—even when we've completed our "balance sheet" and recognized that the price is far too high—we still find ourselves reluctant to let go. This reluctance isn't a sign of weakness or failure. Rather, it reflects the complex relationship we develop with our pain and the many hidden ways it becomes integrated into our lives, identities, and understanding of the world.

In Chapter 2, we explored what staying tethered to our pain costs us. Now we'll examine why, despite these significant costs, we continue to hold on. Understanding these dynamics isn't about generating shame or frustration but about bringing compassionate awareness to our resistance. As the prophet Jeremiah reminds us, "The heart is deceitful above all things, and desperately sick; who can understand it?" (Jeremiah 17:9, ESV). Our own hearts often remain mysterious to us, operating from motivations and fears we haven't fully recognized.

In this chapter, we'll explore four primary reasons we resist healing and remain tethered to our pain:

1. The comfort of the familiar
2. Identity concerns: who would we be without our pain?
3. The hidden benefits our pain provides
4. Spiritual and theological barriers to healing

As we examine these areas, remember that resistance to healing is a universal human experience, not a personal failing. From a Reformed perspective, this resistance reflects both our fallen nature and the complexity of sanctification as an ongoing process. The Holy Spirit works gradually in our lives, often revealing layers of resistance one at a time as we're ready to address them.

By the end of this chapter, you'll have tools to identify your own specific resistance points—the particular reasons you might be holding onto pain despite its cost. This awareness creates the foundation for the practical work of releasing pain that we'll begin in Chapter 4.

The Comfort of the Familiar

The Brain's Preference for Predictability

Our brains are remarkably adaptive organs, constantly working to create order from chaos and predict what might happen next. This predictive function serves us well in many contexts—it helps us navigate complex environments and respond quickly to potential threats. However, this same function can make change difficult, even when that change would ultimately benefit us.

Neuroscientists use the term "homeostasis" to describe the brain's preference for maintaining stable, predictable conditions. When we encounter something new or unexpected, our brains automatically flag it as potentially threatening until proven otherwise. This explains why even positive changes—a promotion, a move to a better home, the start of a healthy relationship—can trigger anxiety and resistance.

This neurological preference for the familiar becomes even stronger when it comes to emotional patterns established early in life. The neural pathways created by repeated experiences become like well-worn paths through a forest—easy and automatic to travel, requiring little conscious thought. Creating new pathways requires significant energy and attention, which is why changing established patterns feels so difficult.

From a Reformed theological perspective, this neurological reality reflects how the fall affects every aspect of our being, including our cognitive processes. What neuroscientists call homeostasis;

theologians might describe as part of our natural resistance to transformation. As Paul writes in Romans 7:15, "For I do not understand my own actions. For I do not do what I want, but I do the very thing I hate" (ESV). This tension between desiring change and resisting it is part of the human condition in a fallen world.

The Reformed doctrine of total depravity helps us understand this resistance not as a personal moral failing but as an expression of how sin affects every dimension of our being. This doesn't mean we're as bad as we could possibly be, but rather that no part of us —including our neurological functioning—remains untouched by the fall. As theologian Louis Berkhof explains in his *Systematic Theology*, "Sin has its seat in the heart of man, and from thence influences the intellect, the will, and the affections, in fact the whole man" (Berkhof, 1996, p. 233).

Yet even in this fallen condition, God is at work. As Paul assures us in Philippians 1:6, "And I am sure of this, that he who began a good work in you will bring it to completion at the day of Jesus Christ" (ESV). This promise reminds us that while our resistance to change is real, God's commitment to our transformation is even more certain. The Reformed understanding of progressive sanctification acknowledges both the reality of our ongoing struggle with sin and the certainty of God's transforming work in our lives.

When Pain Becomes Normal

Another factor that makes change difficult is how quickly we normalize our experience, even when that experience involves significant pain. Like the proverbial frog in gradually heating water, we adapt to deteriorating conditions without fully recognizing the danger they pose.

This normalization happens for several reasons. First, chronic pain—whether physical or emotional—becomes our baseline experience, the background against which everything else is measured. Second, we develop coping mechanisms that help us function despite the pain, creating an illusion that things are manageable. Third, we often lack points of comparison that would help us recognize how unusual or unhealthy our situation has become.

Consider how the Israelites, after being liberated from slavery in Egypt, repeatedly expressed the desire to return to their captivity when faced with the challenges of freedom. In Numbers 11:5-6, they complained, "We remember the fish we ate in Egypt that cost nothing, the cucumbers, the melons, the leeks, the onions, and the garlic. But now our strength is dried up, and there is nothing at all but this manna to look at" (ESV). They had so normalized their oppression that freedom, with all its uncertainties, seemed worse than slavery.

This normalization process parallels what Reformed theology understands about habitual sin patterns. As John Calvin observes in his *Institutes of the Christian Religion*, "The nature of man has not only been wounded and weakened, but so corrupted that it needs to be healed and renewed" (Calvin, 1559/2008, p. 251). Our ability to perceive our true condition becomes compromised, making it difficult to even recognize the need for change.

The Devil You Know

Beyond the brain's general preference for predictability and our tendency to normalize pain lies a specific fear that powerfully reinforces our resistance: the fear of the unknown. There's wisdom in the old saying, "Better the devil you know than the devil you don't." When we contemplate releasing familiar pain patterns, we face the terrifying question: What will take their place?

Our imagination often works against us here, conjuring worst-case scenarios about what might happen if we let go of our protective mechanisms. Someone who uses anger to keep others at a safe distance might imagine becoming completely vulnerable to exploitation if they release this pattern. A person who has structured their life around avoiding certain triggers might envision complete emotional collapse if they begin facing what they've avoided.

These catastrophic thoughts rarely reflect reality, but they feel compelling enough to maintain the status quo. The known pain, however limiting, feels safer than the unknown possibilities that lie beyond it.

Scripture repeatedly addresses this fear of the unknown, offering God's presence as the antidote. In Isaiah 43:1-3, God promises: "Fear not, for I have redeemed you; I have called you by name, you are mine. When you pass through the waters, I will be with you; and through the rivers, they shall not overwhelm you; when you walk through fire you shall not be burned, and the flame shall not consume you. For I am the LORD your God, the Holy One of Israel, your Savior" (ESV).

From a Reformed perspective, this fear reflects a practical limitation on our trust in God's sovereignty. While we might affirm God's control over all things intellectually, our emotional resistance reveals places where this theological truth hasn't fully transformed our hearts. As theologian J.I. Packer writes in *Knowing God*, "Our trouble is not that we doubt what we believe, but that we do not doubt it enough; we do not doubt our doubts" (Packer, 1973, p. 18). True faith means trusting God's character and purposes even when the path forward seems uncertain or frightening.

This trust is grounded in God's providential care—His active governance of all things for His glory and our good. The Westminster Confession of Faith describes God's providence as "His most holy, wise, and powerful preserving and governing all His creatures, and all their actions" (WCF 5.1). When we fear the unknown, we're essentially questioning whether God's providential care extends to the unfamiliar territories of our lives. Yet Scripture assures us that nothing falls outside His sovereign governance.

Your Comfort with the Familiar

Take a moment to reflect on your own attachment to familiar pain patterns. Consider these questions:

- What painful situations or dynamics feel strangely comfortable or normal to you?
- When you imagine releasing these patterns, what fears arise?
- How might these fears be connected to early life experiences?

- In what ways might these fears reflect places where trust in God's sovereignty remains difficult?
- What would it look like to take one small step beyond your comfort zone in this area?

As you reflect on these questions, remember that God's character provides a secure anchor during times of change. Unlike our circumstances, which are constantly shifting, "Jesus Christ is the same yesterday and today and forever" (Hebrews 13:8, ESV). This unchanging nature offers the stability we need to face the unknown.

Identity: Who Would I Be Without My Pain?

Pain as Core Identity

Perhaps the most powerful reason we resist healing is the way pain becomes integrated into our core sense of self. Our identities —our understanding of who we are—are shaped by our significant life experiences, particularly those that occur during formative years. When painful experiences happen early or are especially intense, they don't just affect us; they come to define us.

Psychologists who study narrative identity—how we construct our life stories—have found that we tend to organize our self-concept around emotionally significant experiences. These experiences become reference points that help us make sense of who we are and how we relate to the world. When these reference points involve trauma or profound pain, our very identity becomes pain-defined.

Consider how people often describe themselves: "I'm an abuse survivor," "I'm a divorced person," "I'm someone with chronic anxiety," "I'm the child of an alcoholic." These statements may be factually accurate, but they reveal how pain-experiences have moved from something that happened to us to something that defines us.

From a biblical perspective, this pain-based identity represents a profound case of mistaken identity. Scripture teaches that our true, most fundamental identity is found in our relationship with God. For believers, Paul writes that we are "in Christ" (Ephesians 1:3-14, ESV), a phrase he uses over 160 times in his letters to describe our most basic identity. This "in Christ" identity supersedes all other markers of who we are, including our painful experiences.

Ephesians 2:10 further illuminates our true identity: "For we are his workmanship, created in Christ Jesus for good works, which God prepared beforehand, that we should walk in them" (ESV). The word translated "workmanship" (poiema in Greek) suggests an artistic masterpiece. Our identity is not primarily as victims or survivors of pain, but as God's masterpieces, created with purpose and intentionality.

Reformed theology emphasizes this truth through the doctrine of union with Christ. As John Calvin writes, "We do not, therefore, contemplate him outside ourselves from afar in order that his righteousness may be imputed to us but because we put on Christ and are engrafted into his body—in short, because he deigns to make us one with him" (Calvin, 1559/2008, p. 737). This union means that our primary identity is found not in our wounds but in our relationship with Christ.

The Void of Uncertainty

When pain has been central to our identity for years or even decades, the prospect of releasing it creates a frightening void. If I'm not "the person who survived abuse" or "the child of an alcoholic" or "the one who was betrayed," then who am I? This void can trigger what existential psychologists call an "identity crisis" —a profound uncertainty about one's core self that can feel like falling into an abyss.

Nature abhors a vacuum, and so does the human psyche. Without a clear alternative identity to step into, we often cling to our pain-based identity despite its limitations. The uncertainty of who we might become without our familiar pain feels more threatening than the known constraints of remaining defined by it.

For example, someone who has built their identity around being "the responsible one" in a chaotic family system might resist healing because it would require developing a more nuanced sense of self that includes both strength and vulnerability. The familiar role, though exhausting, provides a clear sense of purpose and worth that would temporarily be lost in the transition to a healthier identity.

From a Reformed perspective, this void reflects our need for a more robust understanding of our identity in Christ. As theologian Anthony Hoekema writes in *Created in God's Image*, "The image of God in man has been perverted but not destroyed by sin... In Christ, however, the image of God is being renewed in us" (Hoekema, 1986, p. 83). Our healing journey involves not just releasing pain-based identity but actively embracing our true identity as image-bearers being renewed in Christ.

This renewal process is described in Colossians 3:9-10: "Do not lie to one another, seeing that you have put off the old self with its practices and have put on the new self, which is being renewed in knowledge after the image of its creator" (ESV). The language of "putting off" and "putting on" suggests an active process of identity transformation that requires both releasing old patterns and embracing new ones.

The Survivor's Medal

Beyond providing a sense of identity, our pain often confers a kind of status or recognition that we're reluctant to relinquish. Having endured significant suffering can become like wearing an invisible medal that says, "I survived this." This survivor status can bring validation, respect, and a sense of accomplishment that feels threatened by healing.

For some, the survivor identity provides a sense of moral authority or special insight. "You can't possibly understand unless you've been through what I've been through" becomes both a shield against criticism and a source of unique value. The prospect of healing can feel like surrendering this special status and becoming "just like everyone else."

This attachment to survivor status often manifests as resistance to letting go of anger or resentment associated with past hurts. These emotions, while painful, can feel like badges of honor—proof that we recognize the injustice we endured and refuse to minimize it. Releasing these emotions might feel like betraying ourselves or letting perpetrators off the hook.

From a Reformed perspective, this attachment to survivor status reflects a misunderstanding of where our true worth and significance lie. Our value isn't derived from what we've endured but from our creation in God's image and our redemption in Christ. As Paul writes in Philippians 3:7-9, "But whatever gain I had, I counted as loss for the sake of Christ. Indeed, I count everything as loss because of the surpassing worth of knowing Christ Jesus my Lord. For his sake I have suffered the loss of all things and count them as rubbish, in order that I may gain Christ and be found in him" (ESV).

Our experiences, including painful ones, are part of our story, but they don't define our worth. True significance comes not from what we've survived but from who we are in Christ and how we respond to His calling on our lives.

Your Identity Attachments

Take a moment to reflect on how your pain might be intertwined with your identity. Consider these questions:

- In what ways do you define yourself by your painful experiences?
- What fears arise when you imagine letting go of this pain-based identity?
- What alternative identity in Christ feels difficult to fully embrace?
- Do you derive any sense of status or validation from your survivor identity?
- How might clinging to this identity be limiting your growth or relationships?

As you reflect, remember that your true identity is secure in Christ, regardless of your past experiences. Healing involves embracing this truth more fully, allowing it to reshape your understanding of who you are and what's possible for your life.

The Hidden Benefits of Pain

Secondary Gains

Beyond providing a sense of identity, our pain patterns often bring hidden benefits, sometimes called "secondary gains." These aren't the primary reasons we developed these patterns, but they become reinforcing factors that make change difficult.

Common secondary gains include:

- **Attention or sympathy:** Pain can elicit care and concern from others that might otherwise be lacking.
- **Avoidance of responsibility:** Pain can provide a legitimate reason to avoid challenging tasks or expectations.
- **Sense of control:** Certain pain patterns (like perfectionism or controlling behavior) create an illusion of control in an unpredictable world.
- **Connection with others:** Shared pain can create bonds with fellow sufferers.
- **Justification for anger or resentment:** Pain can feel like a license to hold onto negative emotions.

Recognizing these secondary gains isn't about blaming ourselves or suggesting we consciously choose pain. Rather, it's about acknowledging the complex ways our pain becomes interwoven with our lives and relationships, creating subtle incentives to maintain the status quo.

From a Reformed perspective, these secondary gains often reflect our fallen tendency to seek fulfillment and security outside of God. When we rely on pain to elicit sympathy, we're looking to others for the unconditional acceptance found only in Christ. When we use pain to avoid responsibility, we're resisting God's call to faithful stewardship of our gifts and opportunities.

Scripture warns against seeking validation through suffering. While Paul speaks of rejoicing in his sufferings for Christ's sake (Colossians 1:24), this is fundamentally different from deriving secondary gains from personal pain patterns. True Christian suffering points others to Christ, while secondary gains often keep the focus on ourselves.

Pain as a Motivator

Sometimes, pain serves as a powerful motivator for positive change or achievement. Many successful individuals attribute their drive to overcoming early adversity or proving doubters wrong. While this motivation can be productive, it also creates resistance to healing. If pain is the fuel for our success, what happens when that pain diminishes?

This dynamic often underlies workaholism or relentless striving. The fear isn't just of failure but of losing the very engine that drives achievement. Healing might feel like settling for mediocrity or losing one's edge.

From a Reformed perspective, this highlights the difference between motivation rooted in pain and motivation rooted in gratitude for God's grace. As the Heidelberg Catechism explains, our good works should flow not from a desire to earn salvation or prove ourselves, but from thankfulness for the redemption we've received in Christ (HC Q.86). Healing involves shifting our motivation from proving ourselves through striving to responding gratefully to God's love.

Identifying Your Secondary Gains

Take a moment to reflect on potential hidden benefits your pain patterns might provide. Consider these questions:

- What positive outcomes, however small, result from your pain patterns?
- Does your pain elicit care or attention you might not otherwise receive?
- Does it allow you to avoid situations or responsibilities you find difficult?
- Does it provide a sense of connection with others who share similar struggles?
- Does it fuel your motivation or drive in any area of life?

Acknowledging these secondary gains requires honesty and humility. It's not about judging yourself but about understanding the full picture of why change feels difficult. Recognizing these benefits allows you to consciously seek healthier ways to meet those underlying needs—ways aligned with God's design rather than rooted in pain.

Spiritual and Theological Barriers

Misunderstanding God's Role in Suffering

Our theological beliefs about suffering significantly impact our willingness to pursue healing. Certain misunderstandings can create powerful barriers:

- **Believing suffering is punishment:** If we view our pain as deserved punishment from God, we may resist healing out of a sense of obligation or fear of defying God's judgment.
- **Equating suffering with holiness:** Some traditions emphasize suffering as a path to spiritual maturity, leading people to passively accept pain rather than actively seeking healing.
- **Doubting God's goodness or power:** If past experiences have led us to question God's ability or willingness to heal, we may lack the faith needed to pursue it.
- **Fear of questioning God:** Some believe that acknowledging the depth of their pain or seeking psychological help implies a lack of faith or questions God's sovereignty.

From a Reformed perspective, a robust understanding of God's sovereignty and goodness provides a foundation for pursuing healing. While God is sovereign over suffering (Lamentations 3:37-38), He is not the author of evil (James 1:13). His purposes in allowing suffering are redemptive, aimed at conforming us to Christ's image (Romans 8:28-29).

Reformed theology also affirms the goodness of seeking healing through appropriate means, including medical and psychological help, as expressions of God's common grace. As the Westminster Larger Catechism states, the sixth commandment requires "all careful studies, and lawful endeavors, to preserve the life of ourselves and others" (WLC Q.135), which includes seeking healing for both body and soul.

Fear of Forgiveness

Forgiveness—both receiving God's forgiveness and extending forgiveness to others—is central to Christian healing. However, fear often surrounds this process:

- **Fear that forgiving others means condoning their actions:** Many resist forgiving perpetrators because they believe it minimizes the harm done or lets the offender off the hook.
- **Fear of vulnerability after forgiving:** Letting go of resentment can feel like lowering defenses that protect against future hurt.
- **Fear of not being truly forgiven by God:** If we struggle with shame or guilt, we may doubt the completeness of God's forgiveness, hindering our ability to heal.

From a Reformed perspective, forgiveness is grounded in Christ's substitutionary atonement. We forgive others because God has first forgiven us (Ephesians 4:32). This forgiveness doesn't require forgetting the offense or reconciling with the offender but involves releasing our right to bitterness and judgment, entrusting justice to God.

Receiving God's forgiveness requires embracing the doctrine of justification by faith alone—the truth that we are declared righteous in God's sight solely based on Christ's work, not our own merit (Romans 3:21-26). Healing often involves a deeper appropriation of this foundational truth.

Identifying Your Spiritual Barriers

Take a moment to reflect on potential spiritual or theological barriers to your healing. Consider these questions:

- What beliefs do you hold about suffering that might hinder your pursuit of healing?
- Do you struggle to reconcile God's sovereignty with His goodness in the face of your pain?
- What fears arise when you consider forgiving those who have hurt you?
- Do you fully believe and embrace God's forgiveness for your own sins and shortcomings?
- How might these spiritual barriers be intertwined with the other forms of resistance we've discussed?

Addressing these barriers often requires deeper engagement with Scripture, theological reflection, prayer, and potentially guidance from pastors or trusted spiritual mentors. Recognizing them is the first step toward seeking clarity and truth.

As we conclude this chapter, remember that resistance to healing is complex and multifaceted. Understanding why we hold onto pain—whether due to familiarity, identity concerns, hidden benefits, or spiritual barriers—allows us to approach our resistance with compassion and wisdom. This self-awareness prepares us for the next stage of our journey: actively challenging the narratives and patterns that keep us tethered.

Worksheet: Examining Identity Attachments

Instructions: Chapter 3 discussed how we can become attached to identities rooted in our pain or limitations, finding a strange comfort in the familiar. Reflect on potential identities you might be attached to. Use the prompts below to explore one such attachment.

   a. **Potential Identity Attachment:**

_____

_____

(Describe the identity, e.g., "The Victim," "The Chronically Ill One," "The Failure," "The Anxious One.")

   b. **What perceived "benefits" or comforts does this identity provide?**

_____

_____

(Consider predictability, sympathy, avoidance of responsibility, sense of belonging with others sharing the identity, etc.)

c. **What are the costs or limitations of holding onto this identity?**

_____

_____

(Think about how it restricts growth, relationships, joy, or living out your God-given potential.)

d. **How does this identity conflict with your true identity in Christ?**

_____

_____

_____

_____

_____

_____

(Consider biblical descriptions of believers: child of God, new creation, forgiven, redeemed, *empowered by the Spirit, etc.)* * *Biblical Truth 1 (e.g., 2 Cor 5:17):* * *Contrast with Attached Identity:* * *Biblical Truth 2 (e.g., Romans 8:1):* * *Contrast with Attached Identity:*

Letting Go:

- What is one small step you can take this week to act in accordance with your true identity in Christ, rather than the attached identity?

_____

_____

- Pray for the Holy Spirit's help to loosen the grip of this familiar but limiting identity and to embrace the freedom found in Christ. "So if the Son sets you free, you will be free indeed" (John 8:36).

PART II
UNTANGLING THE KNOTS

.

FOUR

Examining The Narratives

> *"You will know the truth, and the truth will set you free."*
>
> John 8:32 (ESV)

Have you ever watched a child with a tangled kite string? There's a moment of recognition as they stare at the hopeless knot, wondering how something that started so simply could become so complicated. Some children immediately call for help, others tug randomly at loops hoping for a miracle, while the most patient ones sit down and begin the meticulous work of examining each twist and turn, understanding how the string became entangled before attempting to free it.

In many ways, our journey toward healing follows a similar pattern. In the previous chapters, we've recognized that we're tethered to our pain and acknowledged the significant costs of remaining bound. We've explored why, despite these costs, we continue to hold on. Now we begin the careful, intentional work of examining the specific knots that keep us tethered—the narratives we've constructed about our pain, ourselves, and God.

These narratives aren't simply stories we tell; they're the interpretive frameworks through which we understand our experiences and make meaning of our lives. They operate largely beneath our conscious awareness, shaping how we see the world, ourselves, and our possibilities. When these narratives form around painful experiences, they often become rigid and limiting, keeping us tethered to the past even as we long for freedom.

In this chapter, we'll explore how to identify and examine these narratives as the essential first step in untangling them. We'll look at common pain-based narratives, provide tools for recognizing your own narrative patterns, and examine how these stories shape not only your view of yourself but also your understanding of God. This examination isn't about assigning blame—either to yourself or others—but about bringing compassionate awareness to the stories that have shaped your life.

As Jesus promised in John 8:32, "You will know the truth, and the truth will set you free" (ESV). Truth is the antidote to the distorted narratives that keep us bound. But before we can embrace truth, we must first recognize the narratives we've been living by. This recognition is the focus of our work in this chapter.

The Stories We Tell Ourselves

Narrative Psychology: A Reformed Perspective

We are, by nature, storytellers. From earliest childhood, we organize our experiences into narratives that help us make sense of the world and our place in it. This isn't just a psychological observation but reflects how God has designed us as meaning-making creatures. Throughout Scripture, we see God communicating through story—from the grand narrative of creation, fall, redemption, and restoration that spans the Bible to the specific parables Jesus used to convey spiritual truth.

Narrative psychology, which studies how humans construct and use stories to interpret experience, offers valuable insights that align with a Reformed understanding of human nature. From a Reformed perspective, we recognize that while our narrative capacity reflects God's image in us, our fallen nature means our stories are always subject to distortion. As theologian Cornelius Plantinga notes in *Not the Way It's Supposed to Be*, "Sin is both a wrecking of shalom and a distortion of the way things are supposed to be" (Plantinga, 1995, p. 5). This distortion affects not just our actions but our very perception and interpretation of reality.

The doctrine of total depravity helps us understand why our narratives often become skewed. This doctrine doesn't mean we're as bad as we could possibly be, but rather that no aspect of our being—including our cognitive processes and meaning-making—remains untouched by the fall. As a result, we naturally construct narratives that protect our sense of self, minimize our responsibility, magnify our victimization, or otherwise distort reality in ways that seem to serve us but ultimately keep us bound.

Yet even in our fallen state, God's common grace enables us to recognize truth when confronted with it. As John Calvin observed in his *Institutes of the Christian Religion*, there remains in all people "some seed of religion," some capacity to perceive truth despite our distortions (Calvin, 1559/2008, p. 43). This capacity, illuminated by the Holy Spirit, allows us to examine our narratives and begin to discern where they diverge from reality.

How Pain Shapes Our Stories

Painful experiences have a particularly powerful impact on our narrative formation. When we experience trauma, profound loss, or persistent suffering, our brains work overtime to make sense of what has happened. This sense-making process is natural and necessary—we need some framework to understand our experiences—but it often occurs under conditions that promote distortion rather than clarity.

Several factors contribute to this distortion:

First, pain activates our threat-response system, flooding our bodies with stress hormones that enhance emotional memory while impairing the brain regions responsible for contextual thinking and nuanced interpretation. This means our pain narratives often form when we're least equipped to construct balanced, accurate stories.

Second, childhood pain shapes narratives during developmental periods when we lack the cognitive capacity for complex understanding. A five-year-old who experiences parental abandonment doesn't have the perspective to recognize that the parent's actions reflect the parent's limitations rather than the child's worth. Instead, the child naturally constructs a self-blaming narrative: "I wasn't lovable enough to make them stay."

Third, we often form pain narratives in isolation, without the benefit of community perspectives that might offer alternative interpretations. This isolation may be physical (literally being alone) or emotional (feeling unable to share our true experience with others). Either way, it deprives us of the corrective input that community can provide.

From a Reformed perspective, these factors reflect both our creaturely limitations and the effects of the fall. We are finite beings with limited perspective, and we live in a fallen world where sin distorts both our experiences and our interpretations of them. As Herman Bavinck writes in *Reformed Dogmatics*, "Sin does not just consist in deeds but penetrates to the core of human nature and extends to the whole person" (Bavinck, 2006, p. 83). This includes our narrative construction.

Yet Scripture also testifies to God's redemptive work in human stories. Throughout the Bible, we see God entering into people's distorted narratives and reframing them according to His larger purposes. Joseph's statement to his brothers in Genesis 50:20 exemplifies this reframing: "As for you, you meant evil against me, but God meant it for good" (ESV). Joseph doesn't deny the reality of his brothers' harmful actions but interprets them within God's larger redemptive narrative.

This biblical pattern offers hope for our own narrative examination. With God's help, we can begin to recognize how pain has shaped our stories and open ourselves to the possibility of reframing them according to His truth.

The Power of Implicit Narratives

Some of our most influential narratives operate implicitly—below the level of conscious awareness. These aren't stories we deliberately tell ourselves, but assumptions so deeply embedded in our thinking that we don't even recognize them as narratives. They function as the invisible lenses through which we see everything else.

For example, someone who experienced chronic unpredictability in childhood might operate from an implicit narrative that "the world is fundamentally unsafe." This person doesn't wake up each morning consciously thinking this thought. Rather, it functions as a background assumption that shapes how they approach relationships, make decisions, and respond to challenges. It feels not like a story but like reality itself.

These implicit narratives are particularly powerful because they operate without our awareness or consent. They color our perception before we have a chance to evaluate what we're seeing. As Proverbs 4:23 warns, "Keep your heart with all vigilance, for from it flow the springs of life" (ESV). The heart in biblical terms includes not just emotions but our core beliefs and perceptions—the implicit narratives from which our life patterns flow.

From a Reformed perspective, bringing these implicit narratives into awareness is part of the sanctification process. As Paul writes in Romans 12:2, "Do not be conformed to this world, but be transformed by the renewal of your mind" (ESV). This renewal involves recognizing how our minds have been shaped by painful experiences and opening ourselves to God's transforming truth.

The Reformed emphasis on the sufficiency of Scripture is particularly relevant here. While psychological insights help us identify our implicit narratives, Scripture provides the authoritative standard against which to evaluate them. As 2 Timothy 3:16-17 tells us, "All Scripture is breathed out by God and profitable for teaching, for reproof, for correction, and for training in righteousness, that the man of God may be complete, equipped for every good work" (ESV). Scripture offers both the mirror that reveals our distorted narratives and the truth that corrects them.

Biblical Examples of Narrative Influence

Scripture provides numerous examples of how narratives shape perception and behavior. Consider the Israelites after their deliverance from Egypt. Despite witnessing God's miraculous provision, they quickly constructed a narrative of abandonment when facing challenges in the wilderness. In Exodus 16:3, they complain, "Would that we had died by the hand of the LORD in the land of Egypt, when we sat by the meat pots and ate bread to the full, for you have brought us out into this wilderness to kill this whole assembly with hunger" (ESV).

This narrative distorted both their past (idealizing their slavery in Egypt) and their present (interpreting temporary hardship as evidence of God's intent to harm them). It wasn't based on careful evaluation of evidence but on fear and limited perspective. Yet it felt completely real to them and shaped their responses to their circumstances.

The disciples demonstrate similar narrative distortion after Jesus' crucifixion. Despite Jesus' repeated predictions of His death and resurrection, the disciples' narrative that the Messiah would establish an immediate political kingdom was so entrenched that they couldn't integrate Jesus' actual words into their understanding. This narrative collapse is evident in the words of the disciples on the road to Emmaus: "But we had hoped that he was the one to redeem Israel" (Luke 24:21, ESV). Their narrative of what redemption should look like prevented them from recognizing the true redemption unfolding before them.

Even after the resurrection, the disciples struggled with narrative revision. In Acts 1:6, they ask the risen Jesus, "Lord, will you at this time restore the kingdom to Israel?" (ESV). Their national-political narrative of redemption remained so powerful that even the resurrection hadn't fully dislodged it.

These biblical examples illustrate both the power of entrenched narratives and the possibility of narrative transformation. The disciples eventually embraced a new narrative of God's kingdom that transcended their previous understanding. This transformation didn't happen instantly but through a process of confrontation with reality, community discussion, and divine illumination —the same elements that facilitate narrative examination in our own lives.

Common Pain Narratives

The Victim Narrative: "I Am Powerless"

One of the most common pain-based narratives centers on victimization and powerlessness. To be clear, many people have genuinely been victimized by others' actions or by circumstances beyond their control. The victim narrative becomes problematic not when it acknowledges real victimization but when it becomes a totalizing identity that defines all aspects of life.

The core belief in this narrative is "I am powerless." This belief manifests in statements like: "Things happen to me; I don't make things happen," "I have no control over my life," "Others determine what happens to me," "I am at the mercy of my circumstances."

This narrative often develops from experiences where we genuinely lacked power or control—childhood abuse, systemic discrimination, natural disasters, or other situations where our agency was severely limited. The narrative served a protective function during the original experience, helping us cope with circumstances we couldn't change. The problem arises when this narrative persists long after the original situation has ended, continuing to limit our sense of agency in contexts where we actually have significant choice and power.

From a theological perspective, the victim narrative often reflects a distorted understanding of God's sovereignty and human responsibility. Reformed theology emphasizes God's sovereign control over all things while simultaneously affirming meaningful human agency within that sovereignty. As the Westminster Confession states, God has ordained whatsoever comes to pass "yet so as thereby neither is God the author of sin, nor is violence offered to the will of the creatures" (WCF 3.1).

When the victim narrative becomes entrenched, it collapses this nuanced understanding, effectively denying our God-given agency and responsibility. It can also distort our view of God, portraying Him either as the author of our victimization or as powerless to prevent it. Neither view aligns with the biblical revelation of God as both sovereign and good, working all things together for the good of those who love Him (Romans 8:28).

The Shame Narrative: "I Am Defective"

Another common pain narrative centers on shame and fundamental defectiveness. Unlike guilt, which relates to specific actions ("I did something bad"), shame relates to core identity ("I am bad"). The shame narrative interprets painful experiences as evidence of inherent unworthiness or defectiveness.

The core belief in this narrative is "I am defective." This belief manifests in statements like: "Something is fundamentally wrong with me," "If people really knew me, they would reject me," "I am unworthy of love and belonging," "My needs and feelings don't matter."

This narrative often develops from experiences of rejection, abandonment, or persistent criticism, particularly during formative years. When children receive consistent messages—whether explicit or implicit—that they are somehow inadequate or unacceptable, they naturally internalize these messages as truth about their identity.

From a theological perspective, the shame narrative reflects a distorted understanding of human sinfulness and God's grace. Reformed theology affirms the reality of human fallenness while simultaneously emphasizing God's gracious acceptance of believers in Christ. As Ephesians 1:4-5 declares, God has "chosen us in him before the foundation of the world, that we should be holy and blameless before him. In love he predestined us for adoption to himself as sons through Jesus Christ" (ESV).

The shame narrative acknowledges human brokenness but fails to recognize God's redemptive purpose and gracious acceptance. It sees only our fallenness without embracing the equally true reality of our belovedness in Christ. This partial truth becomes a devastating lie when it stands alone, defining our entire identity.

The Abandonment Narrative: "I Am Unwanted"

Closely related to the shame narrative is the abandonment narrative, which centers on the belief that we are fundamentally unwanted or disposable. This narrative interprets painful experiences—particularly relational losses—as evidence that we are the kind of person who gets left behind.

The core belief in this narrative is "I am unwanted." This belief manifests in statements like: "People always leave," "I'm destined to be alone," "No one will ever truly choose me," "I have to earn love and belonging."

This narrative often develops from experiences of actual abandonment, neglect, or significant loss, such as the death of a parent, divorce, or rejection by peers. It creates hypervigilance about potential rejection and often leads to patterns of either clinging desperately to relationships or preemptively pushing others away to avoid the anticipated pain of being left.

From a theological perspective, the abandonment narrative contradicts the profound truth of God's covenant faithfulness and His unwavering commitment to His people. While human relationships may fail us, God promises, "I will never leave you nor forsake you" (Hebrews 13:5, ESV). The entire narrative of Scripture testifies to God's relentless pursuit of His people, even in their unfaithfulness.

The doctrine of adoption provides a powerful counter-narrative to abandonment. As believers, we are not just forgiven but adopted into God's family as beloved children (Romans 8:15-17). This adoption isn't based on our desirability but on God's sovereign grace. It means our fundamental status is not "unwanted" but "chosen and beloved."

The Fear Narrative: "The World Is Unsafe"

Another pervasive pain narrative centers on fear and the belief that the world is fundamentally unsafe. This narrative interprets painful experiences as evidence that danger lurks around every corner and that safety is an illusion.

The core belief in this narrative is "The world is unsafe." This belief manifests in statements like: "Something bad is always about to happen," "I can't trust anyone or anything," "I have to be constantly vigilant to protect myself," "Safety is impossible."

This narrative often develops from experiences of trauma, unpredictable environments, or exposure to violence or instability. It creates chronic anxiety, hypervigilance, and difficulty trusting others or relaxing. People living within this narrative often structure their lives around minimizing risk, which can lead to significant limitations on their experiences and relationships.

From a theological perspective, the fear narrative reflects a distorted understanding of God's providence and protection. While Scripture acknowledges the reality of danger and suffering in a fallen world, it consistently calls believers to trust in God's sovereign care rather than living in fear. Jesus repeatedly tells His disciples, "Do not be anxious" (Matthew 6:25-34) and "Do not fear" (Luke 12:32), grounding this command in God's loving provision and control.

Reformed theology affirms God's providence—His active governance over all creation—as the foundation for trust in the face of uncertainty. As the Heidelberg Catechism beautifully states, God's providence means He "upholds and governs heaven, earth, and all creatures in such a way that... all things, in fact, come to us not by chance but by his fatherly hand" (HC Q.27). This doesn't mean believers are exempt from suffering, but it does mean that nothing happens outside God's sovereign control and redemptive purposes.

Tools for Examining Your Narratives

Narrative Journaling

One effective tool for identifying and examining your narratives is narrative journaling. This involves writing about significant life experiences, paying attention not just to the events themselves but to the meaning you made of them and the stories you constructed.

Try this exercise:

1. Choose a significant painful experience from your past.
2. Write about the experience as objectively as possible: What happened? Who was involved? When and where did it occur?
3. Now, reflect on the meaning you made of this experience at the time. What conclusions did you draw about yourself, others, God, or the world?
4. How has this narrative shaped your subsequent thoughts, feelings, and choices?
5. How does this narrative align with or contradict biblical truth?

Repeat this process for several significant experiences, looking for recurring themes or patterns in the narratives you constructed.

Identifying Core Beliefs

Our narratives often stem from underlying core beliefs—fundamental assumptions about ourselves, others, and the world that operate largely beneath conscious awareness. Identifying these core beliefs helps reveal the roots of our narrative patterns.

One way to identify core beliefs is through the "downward arrow" technique:

1. Start with a specific negative thought or feeling (e.g., "I'm anxious about this presentation")
2. Ask yourself: "If that's true, what does it mean about me?" (e.g., "It means I might fail")
3. Continue asking this question about each subsequent answer until you arrive at a core belief—a fundamental statement about yourself or the world that feels deeply true (e.g., "If I fail, it means I'm incompetent," which points to a core belief like "I am incompetent" or "I must be perfect to be acceptable")

Common negative core beliefs often fall into categories like: - **Helplessness:** "I am powerless," "I am trapped," "I am weak." - **Unlovability:** "I am unwanted," "I am defective," "I will be abandoned." - **Worthlessness:** "I am inadequate," "I am a failure," "I don't matter."

Once identified, these core beliefs can be examined in light of Scripture and challenged with God's truth.

Seeking Community Input

Because our narratives often operate implicitly, we may need input from trusted others to recognize them. Sharing your story with wise friends, mentors, pastors, or counselors can provide valuable perspective.

Consider asking questions like: "Based on what you know of me, what narratives do you see shaping my life?" "Where do you see me limiting myself based on past experiences?" "How does my understanding of this situation seem distorted to you?"

This requires vulnerability and careful selection of who you invite into this process. Choose individuals who are biblically grounded, compassionate, and willing to speak truth in love (Ephesians 4:15).

From a Reformed perspective, this practice aligns with the biblical emphasis on the church as the body of Christ, where members build one another up in faith and truth (Ephesians 4:11-16). We are not meant to pursue healing in isolation but within the context of supportive Christian community.

As we conclude this chapter, remember that examining your narratives is not about self-condemnation but about bringing hidden patterns into the light where they can be addressed. This process requires courage, honesty, and dependence on the Holy Spirit's guidance. By identifying the stories that have shaped your life, you create the foundation for the next crucial step: challenging these narratives with God's truth and embracing the new story He offers in Christ.

Worksheet: Examining Your Narrative (Deep Dive)

Instructions: Building on Chapter 4, this worksheet guides you through a deeper examination of a specific, persistent pain narrative. Choose one narrative you identified earlier or one that feels particularly strong right now.

Narrative Under Examination: (State the narrative clearly, e.g., "I must be perfect to be loved," "My needs don't matter," "God is disappointed in me.")

Part 1: Understanding the Narrative

- **Origins Revisited:** When and how do you think this narrative took root? Were there specific events, relationships, or interpretations involved?

_____

_____

- **Emotional Core:** What primary emotions fuel this narrative?

_____

_____

(e.g., Fear, shame, guilt, anger, sadness)

- **Physical Manifestations:** Does this narrative show up in your body?

_____

_____

(e.g., Tension, fatigue, specific aches – refer back to Body Scan if helpful)

- **Behavioral Patterns:** What actions or inactions result from believing this narrative?

_____

_____

(e.g., People-pleasing, procrastination, withdrawal, harsh self-talk)

Part 2: Challenging the Narrative

- **Evidence Against:** What experiences, truths, or observations contradict this narrative?

_____

_____

(Be specific. Think about the times when it wasn't true, or qualities you possess that counter it.)

- **Alternative Perspectives:** How might someone else view this situation? How might God view it?

- **Cost-Benefit Analysis:** What are the true costs of holding onto this narrative? What are the potential benefits of releasing it?
  - *Costs:*
  - *Benefits of Release:*

Part 3: Replacing with Truth

- **Core Biblical Truth:** Identify a central biblical truth that directly counters this narrative. (e.g., God's unconditional love in Christ, justification by faith, sufficiency of grace, inherent worth as image-bearer).
  - *Chosen Truth:*
  - *Key Scripture(s):*
- **Rewriting the Narrative:** Rephrase the original narrative based on this biblical truth. (e.g., "Because I am loved unconditionally by God in Christ, I don't need to earn love through perfection," "My needs matter because I am created in God's image," "While I sin, God's grace in Christ means I am forgiven and accepted, not condemned.")
  - *New Narrative Statement:*
- **Commitment:** What is one practical way you can live out this new, truth-based narrative this week? Pray for the Spirit's power to renew your mind (Romans 12:2).

FIVE

Emotional Archaeology

"Nothing is covered up that will not be revealed or hidden that will not be known."

Luke 8:17 (ESV)

Have you ever watched an archaeological dig? There's something fascinating about the careful, methodical way archaeologists work—brushing away layers of soil to reveal artifacts that have remained hidden for centuries. Each object they uncover tells part of a story, helping us understand the lives and experiences of people long gone.

In the previous chapter, we began examining the narratives that keep us tethered to pain. We identified common pain-based stories and provided tools for recognizing how these narratives have shaped your understanding of yourself, others, and God. This examination is an essential first step, but narratives don't exist in isolation. They're intimately connected to emotions—

both those we can readily access and those buried beneath layers of protection and avoidance.

This chapter focuses on what we might call "emotional archaeology"—the careful, intentional process of excavating feelings that often lie hidden beneath our conscious awareness. Like physical archaeologists, we'll work layer by layer, using specialized tools and approaching the process with patience and respect for what we uncover.

Some readers, particularly those from certain Reformed backgrounds, might feel hesitant about this focus on emotions. There's a legitimate concern in Reformed theology about overemphasizing subjective feelings at the expense of objective truth. Emotions can indeed be unreliable guides when they become the primary authority for faith and practice. However, Scripture itself presents a holistic view of human nature that includes emotions as an integral part of how God designed us.

The Psalms, in particular, demonstrate the importance of emotional honesty in our relationship with God. David and other psalmists express the full range of human emotions—from exuberant joy to profound despair, from confident trust to bewildered questioning. Jesus Himself displayed emotions throughout His earthly ministry—compassion for the suffering, anger at religious hypocrisy, grief at death, and anguish in Gethsemane. These biblical examples affirm emotions as part of our God-given humanity, not something to be suppressed or dismissed.

In this chapter, we'll explore how emotions get buried, why accessing them matters for healing, and practical approaches to emotional awareness that honor both psychological insights and biblical wisdom. The goal isn't to elevate emotions above Scripture but to recognize them as valuable information in our healing journey—information that, when properly interpreted in light of God's truth, can lead to greater freedom and wholeness.

The Buried Emotional Landscape

How Emotions Get Disconnected

Emotions serve as our internal guidance system, providing vital information about our experiences and needs. Joy signals that something important to us is being fulfilled. Anger alerts us to boundary violations. Fear warns of potential threats. Sadness indicates significant loss. In their optimal functioning, emotions help us navigate life's complexities and connect authentically with ourselves, others, and God.

However, this guidance system often becomes disrupted, particularly when we experience overwhelming pain or trauma. Several factors contribute to this disconnection:

First, overwhelming emotions can feel physically unbearable, especially for children whose nervous systems aren't yet equipped to process intense feelings. When emotions exceed our capacity to integrate them, the brain naturally employs protective mechanisms to disconnect from the overwhelming experience. This disconnection serves an important survival function in the moment but creates problems when it becomes a habitual pattern.

Second, family and cultural messages often teach us—explicitly or implicitly—that certain emotions are unacceptable. Children who are consistently told "Don't cry," "Stop being angry," or "There's nothing to be afraid of" learn to suppress these natural emotional responses. Religious contexts sometimes reinforce these messages, suggesting that negative emotions reflect spiritual failure rather than normal human experience.

Third, traumatic experiences can create fragmentation between emotions and conscious awareness. The brain's protective mechanisms may store emotional and sensory aspects of trauma separately from the narrative memory of what happened, creating a situation where we intellectually know what occurred but remain disconnected from the emotional impact.

From a Reformed theological perspective, this emotional disconnection reflects both our creaturely limitations and the effects of the Fall. As finite beings, we have limited capacity to process overwhelming experiences. As fallen beings, we live in a world where trauma occurs and where sin distorts our understanding of emotions. Yet God's common grace provides insights into these psychological processes, and His special grace offers the context for healing.

The doctrine of total depravity helps us understand that sin affects every dimension of our being—including our emotional functioning. This doesn't mean our emotions are inherently sinful, but rather that they, like all aspects of human nature, have been impacted by the fall. As theologian Herman Bavinck notes in *Reformed Dogmatics*, "Sin does not just consist in deeds but penetrates to the core of human nature and extends to the whole person" (Bavinck, 2006, p. 83).

At the same time, the Reformed understanding of humanity as created in God's image affirms the inherent value of emotions as part of our God-given design. As Anthony Hoekema writes in *Created in God's Image*, "To be human means to be an embodied soul or an ensouled body" (Hoekema, 1994, p. 217). This holistic anthropology recognizes emotions as an integral aspect of being human, not something to be transcended or suppressed in pursuit of spiritual maturity.

Defense Mechanisms: A Theological Perspective

When emotions become overwhelming, the mind naturally employs various defense mechanisms to protect us from psychological distress. These mechanisms, first systematically described by Sigmund Freud and later elaborated by his daughter Anna Freud, operate largely outside our conscious awareness. While secular psychology views these defenses as purely psychological phenomena, a Reformed perspective recognizes them as reflecting both God's common grace in providing psychological protection and the limitations of our fallen condition.

Common defense mechanisms include:

Repression involves pushing distressing thoughts, feelings, or memories out of conscious awareness. Unlike conscious suppression, repression happens automatically, without deliberate intent. A child who experiences abuse might repress the emotional impact of these experiences, creating a situation where they intellectually know what happened but feel emotionally numb when recalling it.

Denial involves refusing to acknowledge painful realities despite evidence. Someone might deny the emotional impact of losing a job, insisting they're "fine" despite clear signs of distress. Denial serves as a buffer against overwhelming feelings until the person develops sufficient resources to face the painful reality.

Rationalization involves creating seemingly reasonable explanations for behaviors or experiences while avoiding their emotional significance. Someone might rationalize staying in an abusive relationship by focusing on practical considerations ("Where would I go?") rather than confronting the painful emotions involved in acknowledging the abuse.

Projection involves attributing our own unacceptable thoughts or feelings to others. Someone uncomfortable with their own anger might constantly perceive others as angry with them, projecting their disowned emotion outward. This defense protects against the anxiety of recognizing emotions we've been taught are unacceptable.

Intellectualization involves focusing on abstract thinking to avoid emotional connection with experiences. Someone might respond to grief by researching the stages of grief rather than actually feeling their sadness. This defense is particularly common in academic and religious contexts where intellectual understanding is highly valued.

From a theological perspective, these defense mechanisms reflect both God's provision and our fallen condition. As provision, they represent the mind's remarkable capacity to protect itself from overwhelming distress—a form of common grace that prevents psychological collapse when emotions exceed our integrative capacity. As Reformed theologian Louis Berkhof notes, common grace "restrains the destructive power of sin, maintains in a measure the moral order of the universe, thus making an orderly life possible" (Berkhof, 1996, p. 434). Defense mechanisms serve this restraining function in our psychological lives.

However, these same mechanisms also reflect our fallen condition when they become rigid patterns that disconnect us from emotional reality. They represent what Reformed theology calls "noetic effects of sin"—the way sin affects our thinking and perception. When defense mechanisms become habitual, they limit our capacity for authentic relationships with ourselves, others, and God.

Jesus addresses this dynamic in Matthew 9:12-13 when He says, "Those who are well have no need of a physician, but those who are sick... For I came not to call the righteous, but sinners" (ESV). Those who cannot acknowledge their spiritual sickness (through psychological defenses like denial) cannot receive the healing Christ offers. Similarly, those who cannot access their emotional wounds remain unable to bring these wounds to God for healing.

The Consequences of Emotional Disconnection

While defense mechanisms provide important protection during overwhelming experiences, their persistent operation creates significant problems for psychological and spiritual health. Several consequences emerge when we remain disconnected from our emotions:

First, emotional disconnection impairs discernment. Emotions provide essential information about our experiences and relationships. When we can't access this information, we make decisions without important data, often repeating harmful patterns because we can't feel the warning signals our emotions would provide.

Second, emotional disconnection limits authentic relationships. Genuine connection with others requires emotional presence and vulnerability. When we're disconnected from our own feelings, we cannot share them with others, creating relationships characterized by surface interaction rather than meaningful intimacy.

Third, emotional disconnection fragments our sense of self. When significant parts of our emotional experience remain inaccessible, we develop a partial self-understanding that doesn't integrate all aspects of our humanity. This fragmentation creates a sense of internal division and inauthenticity.

Fourth, and perhaps most significantly from a spiritual perspective, emotional disconnection limits our relationship with God. Scripture invites us to bring our whole selves before God—including our emotions. Psalm 62:8 encourages us to "pour out your heart before him" (ESV), and the book of Psalms models this emotional honesty in relationship with God. When we cannot access our emotions, this full-hearted engagement with God becomes impossible.

The Reformed tradition, with its emphasis on the whole counsel of Scripture, affirms the importance of emotional honesty in spiritual life. While some strands of Reformed thought have historically emphasized intellectual understanding over emotional experience, the broader Reformed tradition recognizes the biblical pattern of holistic engagement with God. As John Calvin writes in his commentary on the Psalms, "The Holy Spirit has here drawn to the life all the griefs, sorrows, fears, doubts, hopes, cares, perplexities, in short, all the distracting emotions with which the minds of men are wont to be agitated" (Calvin, 1557/2009, p. 39).

This recognition of emotional life appears throughout Reformed theological tradition. The Heidelberg Catechism begins with the question, "What is your only comfort in life and death?" (HC Q.1) —a question that addresses not just intellectual assent but emotional consolation. The Westminster Shorter Catechism defines faith as not merely intellectual belief but as "receiving and resting upon Christ alone for salvation" (WSC Q.86)—a description that includes emotional trust and reliance.

From this theological perspective, emotional disconnection represents not spiritual maturity but a limitation on our capacity to engage with God as whole persons. The journey toward emotional reconnection, then, becomes not merely a psychological process but a spiritual discipline that enables a more authentic relationship with the God who created us as emotional beings.

Emotions as Messengers

The Intelligence of Emotions

Rather than viewing emotions as irrational disruptions to be controlled, both contemporary psychology and biblical wisdom suggest that emotions contain their own form of intelligence. They provide crucial information about our experiences, relationships, and needs—information that complements rather than contradicts rational thought.

Primary emotions—joy, sadness, fear, anger, disgust, and surprise—each serve specific adaptive functions:

Joy signals that something important to us is being fulfilled. It motivates approach behavior and connection with experiences that promote flourishing. Scripture affirms joy as both a natural response to blessing and a spiritual fruit: "You have put more joy in my heart than they have when their grain and wine abound" (Psalm 4:7, ESV).

Sadness signals significant loss and the need for adaptation to changed circumstances. It motivates withdrawal to conserve energy during the adjustment process and can elicit support from others. Scripture acknowledges sadness as a normal human response: "Jesus wept" (John 11:35, ESV) at Lazarus's tomb, despite knowing He would soon raise Lazarus from the dead.

Fear signals potential threat and prepares the body for protective action. It sharpens attention to danger and motivates safety-seeking behavior. Scripture recognizes appropriate fear as wisdom: "The fear of the LORD is the beginning of wisdom" (Proverbs 9:10, ESV), while also offering comfort for harmful fear: "Fear not, for I am with you" (Isaiah 41:10, ESV).

Anger signals boundary violations or obstacles to important goals. It mobilizes energy to overcome barriers and protect what we value. Scripture acknowledges the reality of anger while cautioning against its destructive expression: "Be angry and do not sin" (Ephesians 4:26, ESV).

Disgust signals potential contamination—physical, social, or moral—and motivates avoidance of harmful substances or situations. Scripture employs disgust metaphors to encourage moral discernment: "So, because you are lukewarm, and neither hot nor cold, I will spit you out of my mouth" (Revelation 3:16, ESV).

Surprise signals unexpected events that require attention and updated mental models. It interrupts current activity to focus on new information. Scripture records surprise as a natural response to unexpected divine action: "And they were filled with great fear and said to one another, 'Who then is this, that even the wind and the sea obey him?'" (Mark 4:41, ESV).

From a Reformed perspective, these emotional functions reflect God's wisdom in human design. As part of our created nature, emotions provide information necessary for navigating a complex world. The Fall has distorted but not erased this aspect of God's good creation. As theologian Michael Horton notes in *The*

Christian Faith, "We are not simply intellects, wills, and emotions, but persons—embodied souls—who relate to God and others holistically" (Horton, 2011, p. 397). Recognizing the intelligence of emotions is part of recovering this holistic understanding.

Listening to Emotional Signals

If emotions are messengers carrying valuable information, then healing involves learning to listen to these messages rather than suppressing or ignoring them. This doesn't mean blindly following every emotional impulse. Rather, it means developing the capacity to notice our emotions, identify what they might be signaling, and evaluate that information in light of Scripture and reason.

For example, feeling angry might signal that a boundary has been violated. Listening to this anger involves acknowledging the feeling without immediately acting on it, then asking questions like: "What boundary feels threatened? Is this perception accurate? What would be a wise, biblically informed response?" This process allows us to benefit from the emotion's information without being controlled by its initial impulse.

Similarly, feeling anxious might signal a perceived threat or uncertainty. Listening to this anxiety involves noticing the feeling and associated thoughts, then asking: "What specific threat am I perceiving? Is this threat realistic? What resources do I have—including God's promises—to face this situation?" This approach transforms anxiety from a paralyzing force into a prompt for thoughtful assessment and reliance on God.

From a Reformed perspective, this practice of mindful emotional awareness aligns with the biblical call for self-examination and discernment. As Paul writes in 1 Corinthians 11:28, "Let a person examine himself" (ESV). This examination includes not just our actions but our internal states—our thoughts, motives, and emotions. The goal isn't navel-gazing but greater self-understanding that leads to more faithful living.

The Reformed doctrine of sanctification emphasizes the Holy Spirit's role in this process. As we learn to listen to our emotions with discernment, we rely on the Spirit to illuminate both the messages our emotions carry and the truth of God's Word. The Spirit helps us distinguish between emotional signals rooted in reality and those distorted by past pain or present sin.

Emotions and the Body

Emotions are not just mental states; they are embodied experiences. Each emotion involves physiological changes—shifts in heart rate, breathing, muscle tension, hormone levels—that prepare us for action. This mind-body connection means that accessing buried emotions often involves paying attention to physical sensations.

Practices like the body scan exercise introduced in Chapter 2 help cultivate this awareness. By systematically bringing attention to different parts of the body, we can notice subtle sensations—tightness, warmth, tingling, numbness—that may correspond to underlying emotional states. For example, chronic shoulder tension might relate to unacknowledged burdens, while a tight jaw could signal suppressed anger.

From a theological perspective, this emphasis on the body aligns with the biblical understanding of human beings as unified wholes. Scripture doesn't endorse a sharp dualism between body and soul but presents them as integrally connected. As Paul writes in 1 Corinthians 6:19-20, "Do you not know that your bodies are temples of the Holy Spirit...? Therefore honor God with your bodies" (ESV). Honoring God with our bodies includes paying attention to the emotional information they carry.

The Reformed tradition affirms this holistic view. The Westminster Confession describes humans as consisting of "a reasonable and immortal soul" and "a body" (WCF 4.2), implying unity rather than radical separation. Healing, therefore, involves attending to both spiritual and physical dimensions of our experience, recognizing their interconnectedness.

Tools for Emotional Archaeology

Mindful Observation

Mindfulness, understood as paying attention to present-moment experience with non-judgmental awareness, provides a powerful tool for emotional archaeology. It involves noticing thoughts, feelings, and physical sensations as they arise without immediately reacting to them or getting caught up in their stories.

Try this exercise:

1. Find a quiet place to sit comfortably.
2. Gently bring your attention to your breath, noticing the sensation of air moving in and out.
3. When thoughts, feelings, or sensations arise, simply acknowledge them without judgment (e.g., "There's a feeling of sadness," "There's a thought about work," "There's tightness in my shoulders").

4. Gently return your attention to your breath.
5. Continue this process for 5-10 minutes.

This practice cultivates the capacity to observe our internal experience without being overwhelmed by it. It creates space between stimulus (the emotion) and response, allowing for more thoughtful engagement.

From a Reformed perspective, mindful observation can be understood as a form of disciplined attention that facilitates self-examination and reliance on God. It's not about emptying the mind but about cultivating awareness of our internal state so we can bring it more honestly before God in prayer. As David prays in Psalm 139:23-24, "Search me, O God, and know my heart! Try me and know my thoughts! And see if there be any grievous way in me, and lead me in the way everlasting!" (ESV). Mindful observation helps us participate in this process of being known by God.

Emotion Journaling

Writing about emotions provides another valuable tool for accessing and understanding them. Unlike narrative journaling (Chapter 4), which focuses on stories, emotion journaling focuses specifically on feelings.

Try this exercise:

1. Set aside 10-15 minutes.
2. Begin by asking yourself: "What am I feeling right now?"
3. Write down any emotions that come to mind, without censoring or judging them.
4. Choose one emotion and explore it further: Where do

you feel it in your body? What thoughts are associated with it? What might it be signaling?

5. Consider how this emotion relates to recent events or ongoing life circumstances.
6. Conclude by offering this emotion to God in prayer, asking for wisdom and guidance.

Emotion journaling helps translate vague feelings into specific awareness. The act of naming emotions reduces their overwhelming quality and makes them more accessible to understanding.

Creative Expression

Sometimes, emotions that resist verbal expression can be accessed through creative means. Drawing, painting, sculpting, music, or movement can provide non-verbal pathways to buried feelings.

Try this exercise:

1. Choose a creative medium you feel comfortable with (even simple crayons and paper will do).
2. Bring to mind a situation or memory associated with difficult emotions.
3. Allow yourself to express whatever feelings arise through the chosen medium, without focusing on artistic skill or creating a recognizable product.
4. Afterward, reflect on the process: What emotions emerged? What did you notice during the creative expression?

Creative expression bypasses the cognitive filters that often block emotional awareness, allowing deeper layers of feeling to surface.

From a Reformed perspective, creative expression reflects our creation in the image of a creative God. As Dorothy Sayers noted in *The Mind of the Maker*, human creativity mirrors, in a finite way, God's creative activity (Sayers, 1941). Using creativity to explore our inner world can be a way of engaging our God-given capacities for healing and self-understanding.

As we conclude this chapter, remember that emotional archaeology is a process, not a one-time event. It requires patience, courage, and compassion for ourselves. Some emotions may surface easily, while others remain buried beneath layers of defense. The goal isn't to force emotions but to create conditions where they can emerge safely and be understood in light of God's truth.

By learning to listen to the messages our emotions carry—even the difficult ones—we gain valuable information for our healing journey. This emotional awareness, combined with the narrative examination discussed in Chapter 4, prepares us for the crucial work of reframing our stories and embracing the freedom God offers in Christ, which we will explore in the next chapter.

Worksheet: Mindful Emotion Observation & Journaling

Instructions: Chapter 5 emphasized the importance of acknowledging and understanding our emotions without being overwhelmed by them. This exercise combines mindful observation with journaling to help you process an emotion you are currently experiencing or one that frequently arises.

Part 1: Mindful Observation (5-10 minutes)

1. **Identify the Emotion:** Name the primary emotion you
   want to explore (e.g., Anxiety, sadness, frustration, joy,
   guilt).
   ○ *Emotion:*

   _____

   _____

2. **Location in Body:** Where do you feel this emotion most
   strongly in your body? (Refer to Body Scan if helpful).
   Describe the physical sensations.
   ○ *Physical Sensations:*

   _____

   _____

3. **Observe Thoughts:** What thoughts are accompanying
   this emotion? Simply notice them without judgment, like
   clouds passing in the sky.
   ○ *Associated Thoughts:*

   _____

   _____

4. **Observe Urges:** Does this emotion create an urge to act in a certain way? (e.g., Urge to withdraw, lash out, distract yourself). Just notice the urge.

- *Associated Urges:*

_____

_____

5. **Breathe:** Gently breathe into the area where you feel the emotion. Acknowledge its presence without trying to force it away. Remind yourself that emotions are temporary messengers.

Part 2: Journaling Reflection

- **Trigger:** What situation, thought, or memory triggered this emotion?

_____

_____

- **Underlying Needs/Fears:** What might this emotion be signaling about your underlying needs, fears, or values?

_____

_____

(e.g., Need for safety, fear of loss, value of justice)

- **Narrative Connection:** Does this emotion connect to any of the core narratives you've identified about yourself or your life?

_____

_____

- **God's Perspective:** How might God view this emotion? Is there a biblical perspective or promise that speaks to this feeling? (e.g., God's comfort in sorrow - 2 Cor 1:3-4; His peace in anxiety - Phil 4:6-7; His forgiveness for guilt - 1 John 1:9)
  - _Biblical Perspective/Promise:_

_____

_____

- **Wise Action:** Based on this reflection, is there a wise, God-honoring way to respond to this emotion or the situation that triggered it?

_____

_____

(This might involve prayer, seeking support, taking practical steps, or simply allowing the emotion to pass with self-compassion.)

- **Prayer:** Talk to God about this emotion. Ask for His wisdom, comfort, and guidance in navigating it. "Cast all your anxiety on him because he cares for you." (1 Peter 5:7)

SIX

Reframing Your Story

"And we know that for those who love God all things work together for good, for those who are called according to his purpose."

Romans 8:28 (ESV)

Have you ever looked at an old photograph through different frames? It's remarkable how the same image can evoke entirely different feelings depending on the frame that surrounds it. A simple wooden frame might emphasize the photograph's rustic elements, while an ornate gold frame might highlight its formal qualities. The image itself doesn't change, but our perception and experience of it shifts dramatically based on the context that frames it.

In the previous chapters, we've examined the narratives that keep us tethered to pain and explored the emotional landscape that both generates and sustains these narratives. We've begun the careful work of bringing awareness to stories and feelings that have operated largely beneath our conscious recognition. This awareness creates the necessary foundation for the transformative work we'll explore in this chapter: reframing our painful experiences within God's larger story.

Reframing isn't about denying reality or minimizing suffering. It doesn't require us to call painful experiences "good" when they clearly aren't. Rather, reframing involves seeing our experiences within a broader context that allows for meaning, purpose, and redemption even in the midst of genuine suffering. It's about expanding our perspective beyond the limited frame of our pain to include God's redemptive purposes that transcend our immediate circumstances.

This process reflects a fundamental pattern we see throughout Scripture. Joseph reframes his brothers' betrayal: "You meant evil against me, but God meant it for good" (Genesis 50:20, ESV). Paul reframes his imprisonment: "What has happened to me has really served to advance the gospel" (Philippians 1:12, ESV). Jesus Himself reframes the cross—the ultimate symbol of suffering and shame—as the means of our salvation and His glorification.

In this chapter, we'll explore the biblical foundation for reframing, examine specific reframing strategies, and provide practical tools for applying these approaches to your own painful experiences. We'll see how reframing isn't just a psychological technique but a deeply spiritual practice that aligns our perspective more closely with God's eternal viewpoint.

As we engage in this work, we'll hold two truths in tension: the reality of our suffering and the reality of God's redemptive purposes. Neither truth negates the other. Our pain is real and deserves acknowledgment. God's redemptive work is also real and offers hope beyond our pain. Reframing helps us hold both truths simultaneously, creating space for healing that honors both our human experience and God's sovereign purposes.

The Biblical Foundation for Reframing

Reframing in Scripture

The practice of reframing—seeing painful experiences within a larger context of meaning and purpose—appears consistently throughout Scripture. Far from being a modern psychological technique grafted onto Christian faith, reframing represents a fundamental biblical pattern for understanding suffering within God's redemptive purposes.

The story of Joseph provides one of the clearest examples of biblical reframing. Sold into slavery by his own brothers, falsely accused and imprisoned in Egypt, Joseph had every reason to interpret his experiences as evidence of abandonment, injustice, and meaningless suffering. Yet after years of hardship, when he finally confronts his brothers, Joseph offers a profound reframing: "As for you, you meant evil against me, but God meant it for good, to bring it about that many people should be kept alive, as they are today" (Genesis 50:20, ESV).

This statement doesn't minimize the brothers' wrongdoing ("you meant evil against me") but places it within a larger context of God's redemptive purpose ("God meant it for good"). Joseph doesn't deny the reality of his suffering but recognizes God's sovereign ability to work through even painful circumstances to accomplish His purposes.

The Psalms frequently demonstrate this reframing process. Many psalms begin with raw expressions of pain, fear, or despair but conclude with statements of trust, hope, or praise. Psalm 13, for instance, begins with the anguished question "How long, O LORD? Will you forget me forever?" but ends with the declaration "I will sing to the LORD, because he has dealt bountifully with me" (Psalm 13:1, 6, ESV). This movement from lament to praise represents a reframing that doesn't deny suffering but places it within the larger context of God's character and promises.

The New Testament continues this pattern. Paul repeatedly reframes his sufferings within God's redemptive purposes. In 2 Corinthians 12:7-10, he reframes his "thorn in the flesh"—a source of persistent pain and limitation—as the context for experiencing God's sufficient grace and power made perfect in weakness. In Romans 5:3-5, he reframes suffering as part of a process that produces endurance, character, and hope. In Philippians 1:12-14, he reframes his imprisonment as advancing the gospel rather than hindering it.

Perhaps the most profound biblical reframing centers on the cross itself. What appeared to be the ultimate defeat—the crucifixion of the Messiah—becomes in God's redemptive plan the means of salvation. As Peter declares on Pentecost, "This Jesus, delivered up according to the definite plan and foreknowledge of God, you crucified and killed by the hands of lawless men. God raised him up, loosing the pangs of death, because it was not possible for him to be held by it" (Acts 2:23-24, ESV). The cross, reframed within God's sovereign purpose, becomes not a symbol of defeat but the ultimate expression of victory over sin and death.

From a Reformed theological perspective, this biblical pattern of reframing reflects several key doctrines:

First, the doctrine of God's sovereignty affirms that nothing happens outside God's control or beyond His ability to use for His purposes. As the Westminster Confession states, God "from all eternity, did, by the most wise and holy counsel of His own will, freely, and unchangeably ordain whatsoever comes to pass" (WCF 3.1). This doesn't mean God directly causes evil—the confession carefully adds that "neither is God the author of sin"—but it does mean that even evil actions fall within His sovereign governance and can be incorporated into His redemptive purposes.

Second, the doctrine of providence teaches that God not only creates but actively sustains and directs His creation toward His appointed ends. As the Heidelberg Catechism explains, providence is "the almighty and ever present power of God by which he upholds, as with his hand, heaven and earth and all creatures, and so rules them that leaf and blade, rain and drought, fruitful and lean years, food and drink, health and sickness, prosperity and poverty—all things, in fact, come to us not by chance but from his fatherly hand" (HC Q.27). This doctrine provides the theological foundation for seeing all experiences, including painful ones, within God's purposeful governance.

Third, the doctrine of redemption emphasizes God's commitment to bringing good out of evil, life out of death, and restoration out of brokenness. This redemptive pattern reaches its climax in Christ's death and resurrection but extends to all aspects of God's relationship with His creation. As Herman Bavinck writes in *Reformed Dogmatics*, "The purpose of redemption is not merely to restore the creation to its original state but to bring it to its highest glory" (Bavinck, 2006, p. 307).

These theological foundations don't eliminate the reality of suffering or provide easy answers to the problem of evil. Reformed theology has always acknowledged the mystery that remains in God's governance of a fallen world. As Calvin notes, "The first thing to be learned is the nature of the knowledge of God which leads to a pious and holy life, not to empty speculation" (Calvin, 1559/2008, 1.12.1). Yet these doctrines do provide the framework for reframing our painful experiences within God's larger purposes, even when those purposes remain partially hidden from our limited perspective.

The Difference Between Reframing and Denial

While Scripture consistently demonstrates reframing as a spiritual practice, it's important to distinguish biblical reframing from unhealthy denial or minimization of suffering. Several key differences separate these approaches:

First, **reframing acknowledges the reality of pain and evil**, while denial attempts to minimize or ignore them. When Joseph says to his brothers, "You meant evil against me," he doesn't pretend their actions were anything other than evil. When Paul speaks of his "thorn in the flesh," he acknowledges it as a "messenger of Satan to harass me" and something he pleaded with the Lord to remove (2 Corinthians 12:7-8, ESV). Biblical reframing begins with honest acknowledgment of suffering rather than attempting to explain it away.

Second, **reframing places suffering within a larger context of meaning and purpose**, while denial treats suffering as something to be avoided at all costs. Reframing doesn't claim that suffering itself is good but recognizes that God can work through suffering to accomplish good purposes. As Romans 8:28 promises,

"We know that for those who love God all things work together for good, for those who are called according to his purpose" (ESV). This verse doesn't say all things are good but that God works all things together for good—a crucial distinction that acknowledges both the reality of evil and God's redemptive purpose.

Third, **reframing allows for genuine lament and emotional honesty**, while denial suppresses authentic emotional response. Throughout Scripture, we see God's people expressing their pain, anger, and confusion in honest lament. The book of Lamentations, many of the Psalms, and Jesus' cry of abandonment on the cross ("My God, my God, why have you forsaken me?") all demonstrate that emotional honesty is compatible with faith. Reframing doesn't short-circuit this process of lament but allows it to unfold within a larger framework of trust in God's character and purposes.

Fourth, **reframing recognizes that meaning often emerges gradually**, while denial demands immediate closure. In many biblical examples, reframing occurs after a significant period of suffering and reflection. Joseph's reframing comes years after his brothers' betrayal. Job's perspective shifts only after extended wrestling with his suffering. This pattern suggests that meaningful reframing often requires time and cannot be rushed. As theologian Nicholas Wolterstorff writes in *Lament for a Son*, "Instead of explaining our suffering God shares it" (Wolterstorff, 1987, p. 80). God's presence with us in suffering often precedes our ability to discern His purposes through it.

From a Reformed perspective, these distinctions reflect the tension between God's revealed will and His secret will—what theologians sometimes call His "preceptive will" and His "decretive will." God's revealed will, expressed in Scripture, clearly identifies evil as contrary to His moral character and commands. His secret will, the full extent of His sovereign purposes, incorporates even evil actions into His redemptive plan in ways that often remain mysterious to us.

As the Westminster Confession states, "The almighty power, unsearchable wisdom, and infinite goodness of God so far manifest themselves in His providence, that it extendeth itself even to the first fall, and all other sins of angels and men; and that not by a bare permission, but such as hath joined with it a most wise and powerful bounding, and otherwise ordering, and governing of them, in a manifold dispensation, to His own holy ends; yet so, as the sinfulness thereof proceedeth only from the creature, and not from God" (WCF 5.4).

This theological framework helps us approach reframing with both confidence in God's redemptive purposes and humility about our limited understanding. We can affirm God's ability to work all things together for good without claiming to fully comprehend how He does so in each specific situation. This balance protects us from both the despair that sees suffering as meaningless and the superficial optimism that denies suffering's reality.

The Role of Faith in Reframing

Reframing painful experiences within God's redemptive purposes isn't merely a cognitive exercise but a profound expression of faith. It requires trusting God's character and promises even when circumstances seem to contradict them. This faith doesn't eliminate questions or struggles but provides the foundation for seeing beyond our limited perspective to God's eternal purposes.

Hebrews 11:1 defines faith as "the assurance of things hoped for, the conviction of things not seen" (ESV). This definition captures the forward-looking, trust-based nature of faith that makes reframing possible. When we reframe our painful experiences, we're expressing conviction about realities we cannot yet fully see —God's redemptive purposes that often remain partially hidden in our present circumstances.

The faith that enables reframing has several key characteristics:

First, it's **grounded in God's revealed character** rather than in specific outcomes. Job's ultimate resolution comes not through receiving explanations for his suffering but through encountering God Himself: "I had heard of you by the hearing of the ear, but now my eye sees you" (Job 42:5, ESV). This encounter with God's character—His wisdom, power, and sovereignty—provides the foundation for Job's changed perspective on his suffering.

Second, it **acknowledges mystery without abandoning trust**. Faith doesn't require complete understanding but willingness to trust God even when His ways remain partially hidden. As Moses tells the Israelites, "The secret things belong to the LORD our God, but the things that are revealed belong to us and to our children forever" (Deuteronomy 29:29, ESV). Biblical faith acknowledges the tension between what God has clearly revealed and what remains mysterious from our limited perspective.

Third, it **perseveres through doubt and questioning**. Biblical faith isn't the absence of questions but the willingness to bring those questions to God rather than turning away from Him. The psalmist models this approach: "How long, O LORD? Will you forget me forever? How long will you hide your face from me?" (Psalm 13:1, ESV). These questions don't represent the absence of faith but its authentic expression in the midst of suffering.

Fourth, it **anticipates future redemption** that may not be fully realized in the present. The "hall of faith" in Hebrews 11 includes many who "died in faith, not having received the things promised, but having seen them and greeted them from afar" (Hebrews 11:13, ESV). This forward-looking dimension of faith allows us to reframe present suffering within the context of God's promises that extend beyond our current experience.

From a Reformed theological perspective, this faith that enables reframing reflects both divine gift and human responsibility. The Westminster Confession describes faith as "the work of the Spirit of Christ in their hearts" (WCF 14.1), emphasizing its origin in God's gracious activity rather than human effort alone. Yet this same confession speaks of faith being "different in degrees, weak or strong" and describes believers as "growing up in many to the attainment of a full assurance, through Christ" (WCF 14.3), suggesting that faith develops and strengthens through active exercise.

As theologian Michael Horton writes in *The Christian Faith*, "Faith is not only knowledge but trust. It is not only believing that God exists and that his Word is true, but trusting in him and his Word" (Horton, 2011, p. 583). This trust, nurtured by the Holy Spirit and informed by Scripture, provides the anchor we need to reframe our painful experiences within God's larger story.

Strategies for Reframing

Cognitive Reframing: Changing Your Thoughts

Cognitive reframing involves consciously challenging and changing the thoughts and interpretations associated with painful experiences. This approach, central to cognitive behavioral therapy (CBT), recognizes that our emotional responses are often driven not by events themselves but by our interpretations of those events.

Several techniques facilitate cognitive reframing:

Identifying Cognitive Distortions: Painful experiences often lead to distorted thinking patterns. Recognizing these distortions is the first step toward challenging them. Common distortions include:

All-or-Nothing Thinking: Seeing things in black-and-white categories (e.g., "If I'm not perfect, I'm a total failure").

- **Overgeneralization:** Drawing broad conclusions from isolated incidents (e.g., "I failed this test, so I'll never succeed at anything").
- **Mental Filter:** Focusing exclusively on negative details while ignoring positive ones.
- **Disqualifying the Positive:** Dismissing positive experiences as exceptions or flukes.
- **Jumping to Conclusions:** Making negative interpretations without supporting evidence (mind-reading or fortune-telling).
- **Magnification/Minimization:** Exaggerating negative aspects while downplaying positive ones.
- **Emotional Reasoning:** Assuming feelings reflect reality ("I feel like a failure, so I must be one").
- **"Should" Statements:** Using rigid rules about how oneself or others should behave, leading to guilt or resentment.

- **Labeling:** Attaching negative labels to oneself or others based on behavior ("I'm a loser," "He's lazy").
- **Personalization:** Taking responsibility for events outside one's control.

Challenging Negative Thoughts: Once distortions are identified, they can be challenged by asking questions like:

- "What's the evidence for this thought?"
- "Is there another way to look at this situation?"
- "What's the worst that could happen? Could I survive it?"
- "What would I tell a friend in this situation?"
- "Does this thought align with biblical truth?"

Developing Balanced Thoughts: The goal isn't necessarily positive thinking but balanced, realistic thinking that acknowledges both challenges and resources, both negative aspects and potential positives. Balanced thoughts often incorporate phrases like "Even though..." or "While it's true that..., it's also true that..."

From a Reformed perspective, cognitive reframing aligns with the biblical call to renew our minds (Romans 12:2) and take every thought captive to obey Christ (2 Corinthians 10:5). It recognizes the noetic effects of sin—how our thinking becomes distorted—and emphasizes the role of truth in correcting these distortions. As John Calvin notes, "True wisdom consists principally of two parts: the knowledge of God and the knowledge of ourselves" (Calvin, 1559/2008, 1.1.1). Cognitive reframing contributes to this self-knowledge by revealing our distorted thought patterns.

Narrative Reframing: Rewriting Your Story

Narrative reframing goes beyond challenging individual thoughts to reshaping the overall story we tell about our lives. It involves consciously constructing a new narrative that incorporates painful experiences but interprets them within a larger framework of meaning, growth, and redemption.

Several approaches facilitate narrative reframing:

Identifying Themes of Growth or Resilience: Look for ways painful experiences have contributed to positive qualities like compassion, endurance, wisdom, or deeper faith. This doesn't justify the pain but recognizes that God can bring good even from difficult circumstances.

Connecting to Larger Stories: Place your personal story within the context of larger narratives—family history, community identity, or, most importantly, the biblical story of creation, fall, redemption, and restoration. How does your experience reflect or participate in these larger narratives?

Focusing on Agency and Choice: Even in situations where external control was limited, look for moments of internal agency —choices made, values upheld, or meaning found. Highlight these aspects in your revised narrative.

Writing from a Future Perspective: Imagine looking back on this period of your life from a future point of healing and wholeness. What meaning or significance might you see then that's difficult to perceive now?

Emphasizing Redemptive Themes: Explore how God might be using or redeeming your painful experiences for His glory and your ultimate good. This requires careful theological reflection and often emerges gradually over time.

From a Reformed perspective, narrative reframing aligns with the biblical emphasis on remembering God's faithfulness throughout history. Scripture repeatedly calls God's people to recount His mighty deeds (e.g., Deuteronomy 6:20-25; Psalm 78) as a way of shaping their identity and understanding their present circumstances within God's ongoing story. Narrative reframing applies this principle to our personal histories, interpreting our experiences through the lens of God's redemptive work in Christ.

Benefit Finding: Recognizing Positive Consequences

Benefit finding involves intentionally looking for positive outcomes or consequences that have emerged from painful experiences. This differs from minimizing pain; it acknowledges suffering while also recognizing that growth or positive change can coexist with hardship.

Potential benefits might include:

- Increased empathy or compassion for others' suffering.
- Greater appreciation for life or relationships.
- Clarification of priorities or values.
- Development of personal strength or resilience.
- Deepened faith or reliance on God.
- New opportunities or directions in life.

Benefit finding requires careful discernment. It should never be used to invalidate someone's pain or suggest that suffering is desirable. Rather, it represents a mature capacity to hold both the reality of loss and the possibility of growth simultaneously.

From a Reformed perspective, benefit finding aligns with the doctrine of sanctification—the ongoing process by which God conforms believers to Christ's image, often using difficult circumstances to produce spiritual fruit (Romans 5:3-5; James 1:2-4). Recognizing benefits doesn't mean God caused the suffering for this purpose but that He sovereignly works through suffering to accomplish His good purposes in our lives.

Temporal Reframing: Shifting Your Time Perspective

Temporal reframing involves changing the time perspective from which you view painful experiences. This can involve:

Looking Back: Compare your current situation to the most difficult point in the past. Recognizing progress made can shift your perspective on present challenges.

Looking Forward (Short-Term): Consider how this situation might look in a few weeks or months. This can reduce the sense of permanence often associated with pain.

Looking Forward (Long-Term/Eternal): View present suffering within the context of eternity. Paul employs this perspective in Romans 8:18: "For I consider that the sufferings of this present time are not worth comparing with the glory that is to be revealed to us" (ESV). This eternal perspective doesn't eliminate present pain but places it within a framework that offers ultimate hope.

From a Reformed perspective, temporal reframing—particularly adopting an eternal perspective—reflects the biblical emphasis on Christian hope. Our hope isn't based on escaping present difficulties but on the certainty of future resurrection and restoration in Christ. As the Heidelberg Catechism affirms, our comfort lies in belonging to Christ "in life and in death" (HC Q.1), encompassing both present realities and future hope.

Applying Reframing to Your Story

Choosing Where to Start

Reframing is a process, not a quick fix. It's often wise to start with less overwhelming experiences before attempting to reframe deeply traumatic events. Consider beginning with:

- A past disappointment rather than a major loss.
- A frustrating situation rather than a traumatic one.
- A specific negative thought pattern rather than your entire life story.

Choose an area where you feel some readiness to explore alternative perspectives.

Using the Tools

Experiment with the reframing strategies discussed:

- **Cognitive Reframing:** Keep a thought journal, identifying distorted thoughts and practicing balanced responses.
- **Narrative Reframing:** Write about a painful experience, consciously looking for themes of growth or resilience. Try rewriting the story from a different perspective.
- **Benefit Finding:** Make a list of potential positive

outcomes or lessons learned from a difficult experience, acknowledging that this doesn't negate the pain.
- **Temporal Reframing:** Practice viewing a current challenge from a future or eternal perspective.

Seeking Support

Reframing often benefits from community support. Discuss your experiences and emerging perspectives with trusted friends, mentors, pastors, or counselors. Their insights can help challenge blind spots and affirm new, healthier narratives.

Small groups focused on healing or spiritual growth can provide a safe context for sharing stories and exploring reframing possibilities together.

Patience and Grace

Reframing takes time and involves setbacks. Some days, old narratives will feel more compelling than new ones. Some experiences may resist easy reframing. Approach this process with patience and self-compassion, recognizing that transformation is gradual.

From a Reformed perspective, this gradual process reflects the nature of progressive sanctification. We are simultaneously justified (declared righteous in Christ) and being sanctified (growing in holiness). This means we live in the tension between our new identity in Christ and the lingering effects of sin and past pain. Reframing is part of this ongoing journey toward greater alignment with God's truth.

As we conclude this chapter, remember that reframing isn't about creating a fictional happy ending for painful stories. It's about discovering the deeper, truer story that God is writing in our lives —a story that acknowledges suffering but ultimately centers on His redemptive purposes revealed in Christ. By engaging in this spiritual practice of reframing, we loosen the tethers of past pain and step more fully into the freedom and purpose God offers.

Worksheet: Reframing Your Narrative

Instructions: Chapter 6 focused on the active process of reframing – consciously replacing old, unhelpful narratives with new ones grounded in biblical truth. Choose a narrative you examined in the Chapter 4 worksheet and the corresponding truth-based alternative you developed.

Old Narrative: *(Restate the narrative you are working on reframing)*

_____

_____

_____

New Narrative (Truth-Based): *(Restate the alternative narrative grounded in biblical truth)*

_____

_____

_____

Part 1: Making the New Narrative Concrete

What does this new narrative look like in action? Describe specific thoughts, feelings, and behaviors that align with this truth-based perspective.

- *Thoughts:*

_____

_____

- *Feelings:*

_____

_____

- *Behaviors:*

_____

_____

Identify Key Scriptures: List 2-3 key Bible verses that support your new narrative. Consider writing them down where you can see them regularly.

- *Verse 1:*

_____

_____

- *Verse 2:*

_____

_____

- *Verse 3:*

_____

_____

Affirmation: Write a short, present-tense affirmation based on your new narrative. (e.g., "I am secure in God's love," "I can face challenges with God's strength," "My worth is not based on my performance.")

Affirmation:

_____

_____

Part 2: Practicing the Reframe

Identify Triggers: What situations, thoughts, or feelings tend to trigger the old narrative?

_____

_____

_____

Develop a Plan: When a trigger occurs, what is your plan to consciously shift to the new narrative? (e.g., Pause and breathe, recall key scripture, repeat affirmation, pray, reach out for support).

- *Step 1:*

_____

_____

- *Step 2:*

_____

_____

- *Step 3:*

_____

_____

Anticipate Challenges: What might make it difficult to maintain this new narrative? How can you prepare for these challenges? (e.g., Discouragement, old habits, external criticism).

_____

_____

Part 3: Seeking God's Help

- **Prayer:** Regularly pray for the Holy Spirit's help in renewing your mind (Romans 12:2) and strengthening your belief in the new, truth-based narrative. Ask God to help you live out this truth.

- **Community:** Share your journey with a trusted Christian friend, mentor, or counselor. Ask for prayer and accountability.

"Do not be conformed to this world, but be transformed by the renewal of your mind, that by testing you may discern what is the will of God, what is good and acceptable and perfect"

Romans 12:2

PART III
CUTTING THE CORD

SEVEN

The Freedom Of Forgiveness

"Be kind to one another, tenderhearted, forgiving one another, as God in Christ forgave you."

Ephesians 4:32 (ESV)

E mbarking on the journey from pain to purpose inevitably leads us to the challenging, yet profoundly liberating, terrain of forgiveness. It is a concept often misunderstood, sometimes trivialized, and frequently resisted, yet it stands as a cornerstone of Christian faith and a pivotal step towards true emotional and spiritual freedom. When the shackles of past hurts, betrayals, and disappointments bind us, forgiveness offers the key—not necessarily to unlock the offender, but to release ourselves. This chapter seeks to explore the multifaceted nature of forgiveness from a Reformed theological perspective. We will differentiate it from common misconceptions that can hinder its practice, outline a practical, grace-empowered process for extending it, and even dare to address the complex and often painful notion of what it means to "forgive God" when our understanding of His ways is clouded by suffering. Ultimately, our aim is to guide you towards embracing the freedom that forgiveness offers, a freedom rooted in the immeasurable grace we ourselves have received.

A Reformed Understanding of Forgiveness

To truly grasp the practice of forgiveness, we must first anchor it in its proper theological soil. From a Reformed perspective, human forgiveness is not a self-generated virtue but a responsive grace, patterned after and made possible by God's own definitive act of forgiving sinners in Jesus Christ. The Apostle Paul exhorts us, "Be kind to one another, tenderhearted, forgiving one another, as God in Christ forgave you" (Ephesians 4:32). This divine initiative is the bedrock of our capacity to forgive. It is not a mere suggestion but a reflection of our new identity in Christ. We forgive because we have been forgiven—an act that cost God the sacrifice of His own Son.

The sovereignty of God plays a crucial role in our understanding and ability to forgive. Both our salvation and our ongoing sanctification, which includes the capacity to forgive, are works of divine grace. It is God who works in us, "both to will and to work for his good pleasure" (Philippians 2:13). Therefore, when we extend forgiveness, especially when it feels impossibly hard, we do so not in our own strength but by the enabling power of the Holy Spirit. This doesn't negate our responsibility; rather, it empowers it. Forgiveness becomes an act of obedience, a participation in the sanctifying work God is doing in our hearts.

Within the covenant community, the church, forgiveness takes on a particular significance. It is essential for maintaining fellowship, resolving conflicts, and presenting a unified witness to a watching world. The bonds of Christian love are strengthened, not weakened, by the practice of mutual forgiveness. It is a tangible expression of the Gospel we profess. When we, as members of Christ's body, extend forgiveness to one another, we demonstrate the reality of God's reconciling love.

It is also vital to understand that biblical forgiveness is not primarily an emotion, though emotions are certainly involved. It is, at its core, a choice and a command grounded in our obedience to God. Feelings of forgiveness may take time to follow the decision to forgive, and that is a normal part of the process. Our commitment to forgive is not contingent on our feelings but on God's clear instruction and the example He has set.

Finally, a Reformed understanding distinguishes our forgiveness of others from God's justifying forgiveness. When God forgives us in justification, it is a legal declaration: He declares us righteous in His sight based on Christ's finished work, imputing Christ's righteousness to us and pardoning our sin. Our forgiveness of others, while reflecting this divine pardon, is a relational act. It doesn't change the objective status of the offender before God, but it does release them from the debt they owe us and frees us from the burden of bitterness. It is an outworking of our justified status, a fruit of the Spirit in the life of a believer who has been profoundly forgiven.

What Forgiveness Is and Isn't

Navigating the path of forgiveness requires clarity. Misconceptions abound, often creating unnecessary barriers or leading to a superficial understanding that fails to bring true healing. It is crucial, therefore, to delineate carefully what biblical forgiveness entails and what it does not.

What Forgiveness IS:

At its heart, forgiveness is **a decision to release bitterness and a desire for revenge.** It is a conscious choice to let go of the resentment that can poison our souls and to relinquish any claim to personal vengeance, entrusting justice to God (Romans 12:19). This doesn't mean the pain magically disappears, but the active nursing of the grudge ceases.

Forgiveness involves **canceling a debt,** whether moral or emotional. When someone wrongs us, they create a deficit, a sense of something owed. Forgiveness means choosing to absorb that loss, much like Christ absorbed the infinite debt of our sin on the cross. It is a profound act of grace, mirroring the grace we have received.

It is also **a commitment to not dwell on or continually bring up the offense against the offender,** especially for the purpose of shaming or punishing them. While the memory may remain, the forgiven offense is no longer wielded as a weapon. This is particularly important in ongoing relationships where past hurts can be easily resurrected.

Often, especially for deep hurts, forgiveness is **a process, not a one-time event.** There might be an initial decision to forgive, but working through the layers of pain, anger, and grief can take time. It may involve repeatedly choosing to forgive as memories or feelings resurface. This is not a sign of failure in forgiving but an acknowledgment of the depth of the wound.

Crucially, forgiveness is **primarily for the forgiver's spiritual and emotional health, freeing them from the bondage of resentment.** Unforgiveness acts like a chain, tethering us to the past and to the person who hurt us. Forgiveness breaks that chain, allowing us to move forward. As Lewis B. Smedes aptly put it, "To forgive is to set a prisoner free and discover that the prisoner was you."

What Forgiveness IS NOT:

Understanding what forgiveness is not, is equally important to prevent us from either demanding too little of ourselves or too much, or from offering a cheap grace that minimizes sin.

Forgiveness is **not forgetting.** The human mind is not designed to simply erase significant memories, especially traumatic ones. We may still remember the offense, sometimes vividly. However, through forgiveness, the memory loses its power to control our emotions and behavior; the sting is removed or significantly lessened. The goal is not amnesia but a redeemed memory.

It is **not excusing or condoning sin.** Forgiveness does not mean minimizing the wrong, pretending it didn't happen, or saying that the offensive behavior was acceptable. Sin should always be called sin. We can forgive the person while still acknowledging the gravity of their actions.

Forgiveness is **not automatic reconciliation.** Reconciliation is a two-way street that requires repentance, change, and a commitment to rebuild trust from the offender. Forgiveness, however, can be a unilateral act. We can forgive someone even if they are unrepentant, are unwilling to change, or even unaware of the depth of hurt they caused. Reconciliation is the ideal outcome, especially within the body of Christ, but it is not always possible or wise if the offending party remains a source of harm.

It is **not removing all consequences.** Forgiveness does not necessarily negate the natural, relational, or even legal consequences of sinful actions. A person who embezzles money and is forgiven by their employer may still face legal charges and will certainly have damaged trust that impacts their employment. Forgiveness deals with the personal bitterness and debt, not necessarily all external ramifications.

Forgiveness is **not trusting immediately or foolishly.** Trust, once broken, must be rebuilt and earned over time, especially if the offense was severe or part of a pattern. It is wise and often necessary to be cautious and to see consistent evidence of change before extending full trust again. Forgiveness can be granted while still maintaining prudent boundaries regarding trust.

Finally, forgiveness is **not waiting for an apology.** While an apology from the offender can be incredibly helpful and can facilitate the forgiveness process, our decision to forgive should not be held hostage by whether or not we receive one. We are called to forgive as Christ forgave us, and He extended forgiveness while we were still His enemies (Romans 5:8-10), long before we offered any apology.

The Process of Forgiveness

Understanding what forgiveness is and isn't lays the groundwork, but how do we actually engage in this often arduous process? While not a rigid formula, several steps, undertaken with prayerful dependence on the Holy Spirit, can guide us toward the freedom forgiveness offers.

First, we must **acknowledge the hurt and sin.** This involves naming the offense honestly before God and, at least, to ourselves. It means refusing to minimize the pain or the wrongfulness of the action. Suppressing or denying the reality of the hurt only prolongs its power over us. Lament, as modeled in the Psalms, is a valid and often necessary part of this acknowledgment.

Second, it is important to **grieve the loss.** Every offense involves a loss—loss of trust, innocence, a relationship, an expectation, or safety. Allowing ourselves to feel the genuine pain, sadness, or anger associated with that loss is a crucial step. Trying to bypass grief often leads to incomplete or superficial forgiveness.

Third, we must **choose to forgive as an act of will.** As discussed, forgiveness is a decision, a conscious choice empowered by the Holy Spirit. This decision may need to be made even when feelings of forgiveness are absent or weak. It is a commitment to obey God's command to forgive and to begin the journey, trusting that feelings may eventually align with the choice.

Fourth, a key element is to **release the offender from the debt.** This can be done verbally in prayer or internally. It means relinquishing our perceived right to hold the offense against them, to demand an apology or restitution (though these may be appropriate in some contexts, they are not prerequisites for our forgiveness), or to wish them ill. We are, in essence, handing the case over to God, the righteous judge.

Fifth, it is immensely helpful to **identify with Christ's forgiveness.** Reflecting on the magnitude of God's forgiveness towards us—the forgiveness of an infinite debt of sin against a holy God—can put the offenses we suffer from others into perspective. If God has forgiven us so much, how can we withhold forgiveness from others (Matthew 18:21-35)? This contemplation fuels our motivation and ability to forgive.

Sixth, Jesus commands us to **pray for the offender** (Matthew 5:44). This can be one of the most challenging steps, especially when the hurt is fresh or deep. However, praying for the well-being, repentance, and blessing of the one who hurt us can be profoundly transformative for our own hearts. It shifts our focus from our pain to God's potential work in their life and ours.

Finally, it is often necessary to **set healthy boundaries,** especially where the offending behavior is ongoing, unrepentant, or where trust has been severely broken. Forgiveness does not mean we must re-enter a harmful or abusive situation without safeguards. Boundaries are not acts of unforgiveness but acts of wisdom and stewardship, protecting ourselves and potentially creating an environment where true repentance and change can occur in the offender.

This process is rarely linear. We may cycle through these steps multiple times for a single offense. The key is persistence, dependence on God, and a commitment to pursue the freedom that lies on the other side of forgiveness.

Forgiving God

Perhaps one of the most perplexing and emotionally charged aspects of suffering is the feeling that God Himself is somehow culpable, leading to the thought, however uncomfortable, of needing to "forgive God." This concept immediately presents a theological challenge: God is perfect, holy, and sovereign; He does no wrong (Psalm 18:30, James 1:13). How, then, can we speak of forgiving Him?

The reality is that this desire to "forgive God" often stems from a place of deep pain, confusion, and a misunderstanding of His nature or His ways. It can arise when we experience profound loss, inexplicable suffering, or witness devastating evil, and we struggle to reconcile these realities with our belief in a good and all-powerful God. The anger or bitterness we feel may be directed at God because He allowed the suffering, because His intervention didn't match our expectations, or because we mistakenly blame Him for the sinful actions of others or the inherent brokenness of a fallen world.

Therefore, the process is less about forgiving God for a fault He did not commit, and more about **reconciling ourselves to His will and His mysterious providence.** It is about surrendering our expectations, our demands for immediate explanations, and our anger at His inscrutable ways. It involves wrestling with our pain in His presence, much like the psalmists did.

The book of Psalms provides a powerful model for this kind of raw, honest engagement with God in times of distress. Psalmists frequently pour out their complaints, their confusion, and their anguish directly to God (e.g., Psalm 13: "How long, O Lord? Will you forget me forever?"; Psalm 22: "My God, my God, why have you forsaken me?"). This is not an act of irreverence but an expression of a deeply personal and struggling faith. God invites us to bring our authentic selves, including our pain and questions, to Him.

The journey of "forgiving God" is ultimately a journey toward **trusting God's goodness and wisdom, even when we don't understand it.** The book of Job is a profound exploration of this theme. Job suffered immense, inexplicable loss, and he questioned God intensely. Yet, in the end, Job's resolution came not from receiving all the answers, but from a renewed and deeper encounter with God's majesty and sovereignty (Job 42:1-6). He learned to trust God beyond his comprehension.

Thus, the path forward involves realigning our perspective with God's revealed character—His love, justice, wisdom, and sovereignty—as seen most clearly in the cross of Christ. It means moving from anger and a demand for our own terms to a humble submission and a renewed trust in His ultimate goodness, even when His purposes are veiled. It is a call to rest in the truth that He is God, and we are not, and that His ways, though sometimes painful and mysterious to us, are ultimately perfect.

Exercise: The Freedom of Forgiveness Worksheet

This exercise is designed to help you practically apply the principles of forgiveness discussed in this chapter. Find a quiet space where you can reflect and write honestly. Remember, this is a process, and it's okay to revisit these questions as needed. Prayerfully ask the Holy Spirit for guidance and strength as you work through this.

1. Identify an Unforgiven Offense: Think about a specific person or situation where you are struggling with unforgiveness. It could be a recent hurt or something from the distant past. Describe the offense briefly.

- Who hurt you?

_____

_____

- What happened?

_____

_____

- When did it happen?

_____

_____

2. Acknowledge the Pain and Its Impact: Allow yourself to feel and articulate the pain associated with this offense.

- How has it affected you?

_____

_____

_____

- What emotions do you feel when you think about this offense? (e.g., anger, sadness, bitterness, fear, shame)

_____

_____

- How has this unforgiveness impacted your thoughts, behaviors, relationships, or spiritual life?

_____

_____

_____

3. Understand Your Resistance (If Any): What makes it difficult to forgive in this situation?

- Are there any misconceptions about forgiveness (e.g., forgiving means forgetting, condoning, or automatic reconciliation) that are holding you back?

_____

_____

_____

- What do you fear losing or risking if you forgive?

_____

_____

_____

4. The Decision to Forgive: As an act of will, and in dependence on God, are you willing to choose to forgive this person/situation?

_____

_____

- Write a prayer or statement of your decision to forgive (e.g., "Lord, with Your help, I choose to forgive [person] for [offense]. I release them from the debt they owe me").

_____

_____

_____

_____

_____

_____

5. Reflect on God's Forgiveness: Take a few moments to reflect on the forgiveness you have received from God through Christ (e.g., read Ephesians 1:7, Colossians 1:13-14).

- How does contemplating God's forgiveness of you influence your willingness or ability to forgive others?

_____

_____

_____

6. Pray for the Offender: Commit to praying for the person who hurt you (Matthew 5:44). What specific things can you pray for them? (e.g., for their repentance, well-being, for God to work in their life)

_____

_____

7. Identify Necessary Boundaries: Does this situation require you to establish or maintain healthy boundaries?

_____

_____

Forgiveness does not mean re-entering harmful situations.

- What boundaries might be wise or necessary for your well-being, even as you forgive?

_____

_____

_____

8. Moving Forward in Freedom: What would it look like for you to live free from the burden of this unforgiveness?

_____

_____

_____

- What is one small step you can take this week to walk in the freedom of forgiveness regarding this offense?

_____

_____

_____

Remember, forgiveness is a journey, often with twists and turns. Be patient with yourself, lean heavily on God's grace, and celebrate the progress you make. The freedom on the other side is worth the effort.

EIGHT

The Practice Of Surrender

> *"Trust in the Lord with all your heart, and do not lean on your own understanding. In all your ways acknowledge him, and he will make straight your paths."*

Proverbs 3:5-6 (ESV)

Following the path of forgiveness, we arrive at another crucial juncture in our journey from pain to purpose: the practice of surrender. If forgiveness is about releasing others from the debts they owe us, surrender is about releasing our own grip —our grip on control, on our understanding, on our will, and on our expectations—into the trustworthy hands of a sovereign God. It is a concept that can feel counterintuitive in a world that often prizes self-reliance and control, yet it is a cornerstone of deep faith and profound peace. This chapter will delve into the biblical understanding of surrender, particularly as an act of active trust in God's sovereignty. We will explore what aspects of our lives we are called to surrender, uncover the spiritual and psychological benefits that flow from this practice, and conclude with a practical exercise to help you cultivate a heart of surrender.

Surrender as Trust in God's Sovereignty

Biblical surrender is far removed from passive resignation or a fatalistic throwing up of hands in defeat. Instead, it is an **active trust in God's wise and good control over all things.** It is a conscious yielding to His authority and His purposes, rooted in the conviction that He is both all-powerful and perfectly loving. Proverbs 3:5-6 encapsulates this beautifully: "Trust in the Lord with all your heart, and do not lean on your own understanding. In all your ways acknowledge him, and he will make straight your paths." Surrender is the practical outworking of this heartfelt trust.

The human heart, since the Fall, is often engaged in a subtle or overt battle for control. We desire to manage our lives, dictate outcomes, and understand every circumstance. This innate tendency clashes with the reality of God's ultimate authority and sovereignty. Surrender, then, is the cessation of this internal warfare, choosing instead to align ourselves with God's reign.

A Reformed perspective on God's providence provides a robust foundation for true surrender. This doctrine teaches that God not only created the universe but also meticulously cares for and governs all aspects of it, including the intricate details of individual lives. Nothing happens apart from His divine decree or permissive will. Understanding that even our pain and struggles pass through the hands of a sovereign God who works all things together for the good of those who love Him (Romans 8:28) allows us to surrender not to a blind fate, but to a loving Father.

Scripture is replete with examples of individuals who modeled profound surrender. Abraham, in his willingness to offer Isaac (Genesis 22), demonstrated ultimate trust in God's command and promise. Job, amidst unimaginable loss, declared, "The Lord gave, and the Lord has taken away; blessed be the name of the Lord" (Job 1:21), surrendering his understanding to God's sovereignty. Mary, the mother of Jesus, responded to the angel's bewildering announcement with, "Behold, I am the servant of the Lord; let it be to me according to your word" (Luke 1:38). The Apostle Paul learned contentment and surrender in all circumstances (Philippians 4:11-13). And supremely, Jesus Christ Himself, in the Garden of Gethsemane, prayed, "My Father, if it be possible, let this cup pass from me; nevertheless, not as I will, but as you will" (Matthew 26:39), providing the ultimate pattern of surrender to the Father's plan.

What We Surrender

The call to surrender is comprehensive, touching every facet of our existence. It is an invitation to unclench our fists from the things we desperately try to control and entrust them to the One who is truly in control. This act of yielding is not a sign of weakness but of profound faith and wisdom. Let us explore some key areas where surrender is paramount.

First and foremost, we surrender **our will and desires.** This is perhaps the most fundamental aspect of surrender. It involves aligning our personal ambitions, plans, and longings with God's revealed will and His greater purposes (Psalm 37:4, Matthew 6:10). It doesn't mean we cease to have desires, but that we hold them loosely, submitting them to God's wisdom and timing, desiring His will above our own. This was the essence of Christ's prayer in Gethsemane: "not my will, but yours, be done."

We are also called to surrender **our understanding and need for answers.** Life is often filled with complexities, pain, and mysteries that defy easy explanation. Trusting God means accepting that His ways and thoughts are higher than ours (Isaiah 55:8-9), and that we may not always understand the reasons behind our circumstances. Surrender here means letting go of the demand for complete comprehension and resting in His infinite wisdom.

Surrender extends to **our fears and anxieties.** The Apostle Peter exhorts us to cast "all your anxieties on him, because he cares for you" (1 Peter 5:7). Similarly, Paul encourages us, "do not be anxious about anything, but in everything by prayer and supplication with thanksgiving let your requests be made known to God. And the peace of God, which surpasses all understanding, will guard your hearts and your minds in Christ Jesus" (Philippians 4:6-7). Surrendering our fears means actively entrusting our worries to God, believing in His care and provision.

We must surrender **our past—our regrets, hurts, and sins.** Holding onto past failures or the pain inflicted by others keeps us tethered to what is behind. Surrender involves releasing these burdens to God's mercy and redemptive power, accepting His forgiveness for our sins, and choosing to forgive those who have wronged us, as we explored in the previous chapter. Paul's mindset is instructive: "forgetting what lies behind and straining forward to what lies ahead" (Philippians 3:13).

Equally, we surrender **our future—its uncertainties and our ambitions.** While planning and working towards goals are good, we must hold our future plans loosely, acknowledging God's sovereignty over them (James 4:13-15). Surrendering our ambitions means seeking first His kingdom and righteousness (Matthew 6:33), trusting that He will guide our steps and bring about His best for us, which may look different from our own preconceived notions.

Our relationships are another critical area for surrender. We are called to surrender our loved ones—our spouses, children, family, and friends—and the outcomes of these relationships into God's loving care. This means releasing our desire to control others, to fix every problem, or to ensure a particular outcome, and instead praying for them and trusting God's work in their lives and in the dynamics of the relationship.

Surrender also encompasses **our possessions and sense of security.** In a world that often measures worth by material wealth or stability, biblical surrender calls us to recognize God as our ultimate provider and the true source of our security. It means holding material blessings with an open hand, willing to use them for His glory and to trust Him in times of plenty and in times of want.

Finally, and perhaps most profoundly in the context of this book, we are called to surrender **our pain and suffering.** This does not mean denying its reality or pretending it doesn't hurt. Rather, it means offering our suffering to God, bringing our brokenness to Him, and trusting that He can meet us in our pain and even redeem it for His purposes and our ultimate good (Romans 5:3-5). It is an acknowledgment that even in the darkest valleys, He is with us, and His purposes will prevail.

The Spiritual and Psychological Benefits of Surrender

The practice of surrender, though often challenging, yields a harvest of profound spiritual and psychological benefits. When we willingly relinquish our perceived control and entrust ourselves to God's sovereign care, we open the door to a deeper experience of His grace and a more resilient inner life. These benefits are not merely abstract theological concepts but tangible realities that can transform our journey from pain to purpose.

Spiritual Benefits:

One of the foremost spiritual benefits is **deeper intimacy with God.** Surrender, by its very nature, fosters dependence. As we let go of our self-reliance, we are drawn into a closer, more reliant relationship with our Creator. We learn to listen more attentively to His voice, to lean more fully on His strength, and to experience His presence in more profound ways. This dependence cultivates a humility that is fertile ground for spiritual growth.

Surrender also leads to **increased faith.** Just as physical muscles grow stronger with exercise, our faith muscles are strengthened each time we choose to surrender. Stepping out in trust, especially when circumstances are uncertain or frightening, stretches our faith and allows us to witness God's faithfulness in new dimensions. Each act of surrender builds a history of God's provision and care, fortifying our belief in His promises.

A significant fruit of surrender is **spiritual peace and rest.** Jesus invites the weary and burdened to come to Him, promising rest for their souls (Matthew 11:28-30). This rest is found in surrendering our striving, our anxieties, and our attempts to control outcomes. When we entrust our burdens to Him, we experience a peace that surpasses understanding (Philippians 4:7), a calm assurance that He is in control, even amidst life's storms.

Furthermore, surrender brings about **alignment with God's purposes.** When our will is yielded to His, we become more pliable instruments in His hands, more readily available to be used for His kingdom's purposes. Our lives begin to reflect His priorities rather than our own, leading to a greater sense of meaning and contribution to something eternal. We move from fighting against His current to flowing with it.

Finally, surrender cultivates **growth in humility.** It requires us to acknowledge our limitations, our finite understanding, and our inability to control every aspect of our lives. This recognition of God's limitlessness and our own finitude is the essence of humility, a virtue highly prized in Scripture and essential for receiving God's grace (James 4:6).

Psychological Benefits:

While the primary aim of surrender is spiritual, it often yields significant psychological benefits as well, frequently as byproducts of a healthier spiritual state.

One of the most notable is **reduced anxiety and stress.** The constant effort to control circumstances, predict the future, and manage every detail of life is exhausting and anxiety-provoking. Surrendering these burdens to God alleviates this pressure, leading to a calmer mental and emotional state.

Surrender can also foster **increased emotional resilience.** When we are not expending all our energy trying to control the uncontrollable, we have more emotional resources to cope with adversity. Trusting in God's sovereignty provides a stable anchor in turbulent times, allowing us to navigate challenges with greater strength and equanimity.

It promotes a **greater sense of acceptance.** There are many things in life we cannot change—past events, the actions of others, certain limitations. Surrender helps us to accept these realities without being defined or defeated by them. This acceptance is not passive resignation but an active choice to trust God within the given circumstances.

Surrender can lead to **improved decision-making.** When our decisions are less driven by fear, the need to control, or self-will, we are able to make choices that are more aligned with wisdom and our core values. We become less reactive and more responsive to God's leading.

Ultimately, the practice of surrender can lead to an **enhanced sense of meaning and purpose.** By aligning our lives with God's will, we find a purpose that transcends our immediate circumstances and personal ambitions. We discover the profound satisfaction of participating in God's larger redemptive story, finding meaning even in our struggles as we entrust them to Him.

These spiritual and psychological benefits are deeply intertwined, each reinforcing the other, creating a virtuous cycle of trust, peace, and growth as we learn to continually practice the art of surrendering.

Exercise: The Practice of Surrender Worksheet

This worksheet is designed to guide you through the practical steps of surrendering a specific area of your life to God. Find a quiet time and space for reflection, and approach this exercise with prayer, asking the Holy Spirit for honesty, courage, and a deeper trust in God.

1. Identify an Area of Struggle for Control: Prayerfully consider an area in your life where you are currently struggling to surrender control to God. This could be a relationship, a career situation, a financial concern, a specific fear, a past hurt you can't let go of, an unfulfilled desire, or a future uncertainty.

- The specific area I am struggling to surrender is:

_____

_____

2. Acknowledge What is Being Held Onto: Explore what you are holding onto in this situation.

What fears, desires, expectations, or beliefs make it difficult to let go and trust God fully in this area?

_____

_____

- My fears related to surrendering this are:

_____

_____

- My desires or expectations I am clinging to are:

_____

_____

- The beliefs that make surrendering difficult here are:

_____

_____

3. List the Costs of Not Surrendering: Reflect on the impact of holding onto control in this area.

- What are the spiritual, emotional, relational, or even physical costs of your resistance to surrender?

_____

_____

- Spiritually, if not surrendering this costs me:

_____

_____

_____

- Emotionally, it costs me:

_____

_____

_____

- Relationally (with God or others), it costs me:

_____

_____

_____

- Physically (e.g., stress symptoms), it costs me:

_____

_____

_____

4. Reflect on God's Sovereignty and Goodness in This Area: Spend some time meditating on God's character, particularly His sovereignty, wisdom, love, and faithfulness, as they relate to this specific area of struggle. Consider the following Scriptures or others that come to mind:

- Proverbs 3:5-6: "Trust in the Lord with all your heart, and do not lean on your own understanding. In all your ways acknowledge him, and he will make straight your paths."
- Romans 8:28: "And we know that for those who love God all things work together for good, for those who are called according to his purpose."
- Jeremiah 29:11: "For I know the plans I have for you, declares the Lord, plans for welfare and not for evil, to give you a future and a hope."
- 1 Peter 5:7: "Casting all your anxieties on him, because he cares for you."

- How do these truths about God apply to my specific struggle?

_____

_____

_____

_____

5. The Act of Surrender (A Prayer or Declaration): In your own words, write a prayer or a declaration of surrender to God concerning this specific area. Be as honest and specific as possible.

Example: "Lord God, I confess my struggle to control [specific area]. I acknowledge my fear of [specific fear] and my desire for [specific outcome]. Today, I choose to surrender [specific area] into Your loving and sovereign hands. I trust Your wisdom, Your timing, and Your purposes. Help me to release my grip and rest in Your care. Amen."

- My prayer/declaration of surrender:

_____

_____

_____

6. Identify One Action Step: What is one concrete action you can take this week that reflects your decision to surrender this area to God? This might be an action of trust, letting go, or changing a behavior that stems from your need for control. My action step is:

_____

_____

7. Ongoing Practice: Surrender is often an ongoing practice rather than a one-time event. How can you continue to cultivate a heart of surrender in this area and in your life generally?

_____

_____

Embracing the practice of surrender is a journey of faith, humility, and growing trust. It is in letting go that we often find ourselves most securely held by the One who loves us perfectly and whose plans for us are good.

NINE

Building A New Identity

"Therefore, if anyone is in Christ, he is a new creation. The old has passed away; behold, the new has come."

2 Corinthians 5:17 (ESV)

As we journey further from the initial grip of pain, having explored the liberating paths of forgiveness and surrender, we arrive at a foundational aspect of lasting healing: the rebuilding of our identity. Pain, especially when chronic or traumatic, does more than inflict physical or emotional wounds; it often insidiously distorts our perception of who we are. The narratives we internalize during seasons of suffering can become deeply ingrained, shaping our self-view in ways that hinder our growth and obscure the truth of our being. This chapter is dedicated to understanding these identity distortions, rediscovering the unshakable foundation of our biblical identity in Christ, learning how to integrate our past pain into this redeemed identity, and engaging in a practical exercise to actively build and affirm this new, true self.

Identity Distortions from Pain

Suffering has a way of speaking to us, and often, its voice is a liar, whispering destructive narratives about our worth, our capabilities, and our future. When pain becomes a constant companion, it can begin to feel like the most defining aspect of our existence. This is where identity distortions take root.

Trauma and chronic pain often shape self-perception by creating powerful, negative internal narratives. A person enduring long-term illness might begin to believe, "I am nothing but my sickness," or "I am a burden to those I love." Someone who has experienced deep betrayal might internalize, "I am unlovable," or "I can never trust anyone, including myself." These are not just fleeting thoughts; they can become core beliefs, lenses through which all of life is viewed. The pain, in effect, hands us a distorted mirror, and we begin to mistake the reflection for reality.

These pain-induced narratives lead to internalized labels and beliefs that can become deeply entrenched, often operating at a subconscious level. We might not even be fully aware of how profoundly these beliefs are shaping our reactions and choices. For example, a childhood marked by criticism can lead to an adult identity built around the label "not good enough," driving a relentless perfectionism or a paralyzing fear of failure. The pain of rejection can forge an identity of "outsider," leading to social withdrawal or an intense need for validation.

The behavioral manifestations of a distorted identity are varied and often detrimental. If we see ourselves as fundamentally flawed or damaged, we might engage in self-sabotaging behaviors. If our identity is wrapped up in being a victim, we might struggle to take responsibility or embrace agency in our lives. Distorted self-perceptions can lead to unhealthy coping mechanisms such as addiction, eating disorders, or codependency. They can manifest in relationship patterns characterized by fear, insecurity, people-pleasing, or an inability to form healthy attachments.

This creates a vicious cycle: the pain fosters a distorted identity, and this distorted identity, in turn, can perpetuate or even exacerbate the suffering. If we believe we are unworthy of care, we may neglect our own needs. If we believe we are defined by our past failures, we may be too afraid to risk future endeavors. Breaking this cycle requires a conscious and deliberate effort to dismantle the false identity constructed by pain and to rebuild on the solid ground of biblical truth.

Biblical Identity Formation

Against the backdrop of pain-induced distortions, Scripture offers a radically different and life-giving foundation for our identity. Understanding who God declares us to be is paramount to dismantling the lies of the past and building a future grounded in truth. Biblical identity formation is not about self-improvement or positive thinking alone; it is about receiving and living out the new identity graciously bestowed upon us through Christ.

At the very outset, we affirm that every human being is **created in God's image (Imago Dei)** (Genesis 1:26-27). This truth confers intrinsic worth, dignity, and purpose upon every individual, regardless of their experiences, abilities, or suffering. Our value is not derived from what we do, what we have, or what has been done to us, but from the fact that we bear the mark of our Creator. This is the bedrock of human dignity.

However, we must also acknowledge our **fallen and sinful nature.** The biblical narrative is clear that humanity, through sin, has marred the image of God (Romans 3:23). This universal human condition affects our identity, leading to brokenness, alienation from God, and a propensity towards self-centeredness. Recognizing this fallenness is not to induce shame, but to highlight our profound need for redemption and to appreciate the depth of God's grace.

It is in Christ that our true and ultimate identity is found. This **identity in Christ** is the core of Christian self-understanding, a multi-faceted jewel reflecting God's redemptive work:

- **Justified:** Through faith in Jesus Christ, we are declared righteous in God's sight (Romans 5:1). Our sins are forgiven, and Christ's perfect righteousness is imputed to us. We are no longer defined by our failures or sins but by Christ's perfection.
- **Adopted:** We are welcomed into God's family as His beloved children, heirs with Christ, sharing in His inheritance (Romans 8:15-17, Galatians 4:4-7). This means we have a Father who loves us unconditionally and a secure place in His eternal family.
- **Redeemed:** We have been bought back from the slavery of sin and its devastating power by the precious blood of Christ (Ephesians 1:7). This redemption frees us to live for God.
- **New Creation:** In Christ, the old has passed away; behold, all things have become new (2 Corinthians 5:17). We are not merely patched-up versions of our old selves

but are fundamentally transformed, with a new nature and a new destiny.

- **Saints:** We are set apart by God and for God's holy purposes (1 Corinthians 1:2). This is not about our own achieved holiness but about our status as those consecrated to Him.
- **Beloved:** We are deeply and unconditionally loved by God (1 John 3:1). His love is not dependent on our performance or worthiness but flows from His very nature.
- **Secure:** Our ultimate identity and eternal destiny are secure in Christ, hidden with Him in God (Colossians 3:3). This security is not shaken by our circumstances, our feelings, or our struggles.

The **Holy Spirit plays a vital role** in this identity formation. He is the one who regenerates us, seals us, and empowers us to live out this new identity in Christ (Romans 8, Galatians 5:22-23). It is through His indwelling presence that these truths move from being intellectual concepts to lived realities.

Finally, **community is essential in identity formation.** The church, the body of Christ, is designed to be a place where our true identity in Christ is affirmed, nurtured, and lived out in fellowship with other believers. It is within this community of faith that we encourage one another, hold each other accountable, and collectively reflect the multifaceted wisdom of God.

Understanding and embracing these biblical truths about our identity is not a one-time event but an ongoing process of renewing our minds (Romans 12:2) and allowing God's Word to define us more deeply than our pain ever could.

Integrating Past Pain into a Redeemed Identity

Understanding our new identity in Christ is crucial, but how do we integrate our past pain into this new reality? It is not about erasing the past, as if it never happened, nor is it about dwelling in it. Rather, integration involves acknowledging the reality of our suffering while reframing it through the lens of God's sovereign, redemptive work and our secure position in Christ. This process allows our past pain to become not a defining scar that limits us, but a part of our story that, when surrendered to God, can deepen our compassion, strengthen our faith, and uniquely equip us for His purposes.

One of the first steps in integrating past pain is **acknowledging its reality and impact without letting it define our core being.** We must be honest about the wounds we have sustained—the losses, the betrayals, the disappointments. Suppressing or minimizing pain only prolongs its power over us. However, while acknowledging the pain, we simultaneously affirm that it is not the sum total of who we are. Our identity in Christ is far more foundational and enduring than any suffering we have experienced.

Next, we must actively engage in **seeing our pain through the lens of God's sovereignty and redemptive purposes.** This is perhaps one of the most challenging aspects of Reformed theology in practice, yet it is profoundly liberating. The Bible consistently teaches that God is able to work all things, including our deepest hurts, together for the good of those who love Him and are called according to His purpose (Romans 8:28). Joseph's declaration to his brothers, "As for you, you meant evil against me, but God meant it for good" (Genesis 50:20), is a powerful testament to this truth. This perspective does not negate the evil or the pain, but it places it within the larger framework of God's ultimate control and good intentions for His children. It allows us to ask not just "Why did this happen?" but also "How might God be using this for His glory and my sanctification?"

This leads to the development of a **"redemptive narrative."** We begin to understand how our personal story, with all its painful chapters, fits into God's grand, overarching story of redemption. Our suffering, when viewed through this lens, can be seen as a means through which God has shaped us, taught us, and drawn us closer to Himself. It can become a platform for a unique testimony to His grace, comfort, and strength.

The process also involves **mourning our losses while simultaneously embracing our new life in Christ.** It is vital to grieve what was lost due to pain—perhaps innocence, trust, opportunities, or relationships. Grief is a healthy and necessary response to loss. However, this grieving should not lead to despair but should be coupled with an active embrace of the new identity, new hope, and new possibilities that are ours in Christ. We look back with honesty but forward with hope.

Finally, integrating past pain often transforms it into a source of **testimony and witness.** When we have experienced God's comfort and healing in our own suffering, we are uniquely equipped to minister to others who are walking similar paths (2 Corinthians 1:3-4). Our integrated pain, no longer a source of shame or defeat, becomes a powerful testament to God's sustaining grace and His ability to bring beauty from ashes. The Kintsugi analogy is apt here: the Japanese art of repairing broken pottery with lacquer mixed with powdered gold, silver, or platinum. The breaks are not hidden but are highlighted, becoming part of the object's unique history and beauty. Similarly, God can take the broken pieces of our lives and, through His redemptive work, make them part of a beautiful and compelling testimony to His grace.

This integration is a journey, often lifelong, requiring patience, prayer, and a continual returning to the truth of God's Word. It is about allowing Christ to redefine us, so that our pain becomes a part of our story, but not the defining feature of our identity.

Exercise: Building Your True Identity Worksheet

This worksheet is designed to help you actively engage in understanding and embracing your true identity in Christ, especially in contrast to any pain-induced distortions you may have internalized. Approach this prayerfully, asking the Holy Spirit to reveal truth and to renew your mind.

1. Identify Pain-Induced Identity Distortions: Reflect on how past or present pain may have shaped your self-perception. What negative labels or beliefs about yourself have emerged from your suffering?

- Some negative labels or beliefs I've internalized due to pain are:

_____

_____

- How have these beliefs impacted my thoughts, feelings, and behaviors?

_____

_____

2. Counter with Biblical Truth about Your Identity in Christ: For each negative label or belief you identified, find a corresponding biblical truth about your identity in Christ (refer to the "Biblical Identity Formation" section or other Scriptures).

Negative Belief: _____ **Biblical Truth:** _____

(e.g., Negative: "I am worthless." Truth: "I am created in God's image and deeply loved by Him – Genesis 1:27, 1 John 3:1")

Negative Belief: _____ **Biblical Truth:** _____

Negative Belief: _____ **Biblical Truth:** _____

3. Meditate on a Key Identity Scripture: Choose one or two biblical statements about your identity in Christ that particularly resonate with you or speak against a strong negative belief. Write them down and spend some time meditating on their meaning and implications for your life.

- Scripture(s):

_____

_____

- What does this truth mean for me personally?

_____

_____

4. Affirm Your True Identity: Write a series of "I am" statements based on your biblical identity in Christ. These should be positive affirmations of truth. * Examples: "I am a beloved child of God." "I am forgiven and redeemed." "I am a new creation in Christ." "I am secure in His love."

- My "I am" statements:

_____

_____

_____

5. Identify One Action to Live Out Your True Identity: Based on your true identity in Christ, what is one concrete action you can take this week that reflects this identity, rather than acting out of a pain-induced distortion? * Example: If a negative belief is "I am not capable," an action might be to step out and try something new that you've been afraid to do, trusting in God's strength.

- My action step is:

_____

_____

- How will this action reflect my true identity in Christ?

_____

_____

6. Prayer for Transformation: Write a short prayer asking God to help you dismantle the false identities shaped by pain and to live more fully in the truth of who you are in Christ. *

_____

_____

_____

Building a new identity in Christ is a transformative process that requires ongoing attention and intentionality. As you consistently replace the lies of pain with the truth of God's Word, you will find yourself standing on more solid ground, increasingly defined by His love and grace rather than your suffering.

PART IV
FLYING FREE

TEN

Creating Meaningful Connections

"A new commandment I give to you, that you love one another: just as I have loved you, you also are to love one another."

John 13:34 (ESV)

Having navigated the essential landscapes of forgiveness, surrender, and the rebuilding of identity, our journey from pain to purpose now turns towards the vital realm of relationships. Past pain, as we have seen, rarely stays confined to our inner world; it inevitably spills over, shaping, and often distorting, how we connect with others. Meaningful, healthy connections are not just desirable; they are a God-given necessity for human flourishing and a reflection of our Trinitarian God who exists in perfect community. This chapter will explore how past hurts can create unhealthy relationship patterns, delve into the rich biblical principles that guide us towards healthy connections, offer practical wisdom on building a supportive community, and conclude with an exercise designed to help you cultivate the meaningful connections you were created for.

Relationship Patterns from Pain

Our past experiences, particularly those involving pain, betrayal, or relational trauma, act as powerful sculptors of our relational blueprint. Without conscious awareness and intentional effort, we often carry the imprints of these experiences into our present connections, leading to patterns that can hinder intimacy, foster misunderstanding, and perpetuate cycles of hurt. Recognizing these patterns is the first step towards breaking free from them and building healthier ways of relating.

Several common maladaptive patterns can emerge from a backdrop of pain:

- **Avoidance/Withdrawal:** If past relationships have been sources of significant pain or disappointment, a natural, albeit ultimately unhelpful, response is to withdraw. The fear of further hurt can lead to emotional distancing, a reluctance to engage in deep connections, or even social isolation. The subconscious thought might be, "If I don't let anyone close, I can't be hurt again."
- **Anxious Attachment/Clinginess:** Conversely, if past pain involved abandonment or inconsistent care, an individual might develop an anxious attachment style. This can manifest as clinginess, a constant need for reassurance, jealousy, or an intense fear of being left alone. The underlying fear is often a deep-seated belief that they are not truly lovable or that relationships are inherently unstable.

- **Mistrust/Suspicion:** Betrayal or deception in past relationships can breed a pervasive mistrust of others. It becomes difficult to open up, to be vulnerable, or to believe that others are genuine in their intentions. A cynical or suspicious outlook can become a protective shield, but one that also keeps out the possibility of genuine connection.

- **People-Pleasing:** Stemming from insecurity or a fear of rejection, people-pleasing involves consistently prioritizing others' needs and desires above one's own, often to an unhealthy degree. While serving others is biblical, people-pleasing is driven by a need for validation or an attempt to avoid conflict or disapproval, often at the cost of one's own well-being and authenticity.

- **Conflict-Driven or Controlling Behaviors:** Some individuals, having experienced powerlessness or chaos in past painful situations, may unconsciously attempt to control their current relationships. This can manifest as being overly critical, demanding, easily angered, or instigating conflict as a way to manage anxiety or assert dominance. Alternatively, they might be drawn to or recreate tumultuous relationship dynamics that feel familiar, even if destructive.

- **Difficulty with Vulnerability:** Vulnerability is the bedrock of true intimacy, but it requires a sense of safety. If past pain involved being shamed, exploited, or hurt when vulnerable, an individual may build strong defenses against showing their true selves, their needs, or their weaknesses. This can lead to superficial relationships where true connection is impossible.

Often, these patterns contribute to a **cycle of re-enactment,** where we unconsciously recreate past painful relationship dynamics. We might be drawn to people who treat us in ways that echo past hurts, or we might behave in ways that elicit familiar negative responses from others. This is not a conscious choice but a powerful pull towards the known, even if the known is painful.

Furthermore, our **impact on our relationship with God** cannot be overlooked. Distorted views of human relationships, particularly with authority figures or caregivers, can be projected onto our perception of God. If earthly fathers were absent or harsh, it might be difficult to embrace God as a loving, present Father. If trust was repeatedly broken by humans, trusting God's promises can feel like an insurmountable leap. Recognizing these projections is crucial for healing both our human connections and our divine one.

Understanding these patterns is not about assigning blame but about gaining insight. With insight, empowered by the Holy Spirit and grounded in biblical truth, we can begin to dismantle these unhealthy ways of relating and build new foundations for connection.

Biblical Principles for Healthy Relationships

Against the backdrop of these often-painful relational patterns, Scripture offers a profound and healing vision for human connection. God, in His very being as Trinity, exists in perfect, loving relationship, and He has designed us, His image-bearers, for communion with Himself and with one another. Biblical principles for healthy relationships are not merely helpful tips but are rooted in God's character and His redemptive plan for humanity. Embracing these principles is key to transforming our connections from sources of pain into channels of grace, growth, and mutual edification.

Love as the Foundation (1 Corinthians 13, John 13:34-35): The cornerstone of all healthy Christian relationships is *agape* love. This is not a sentimental emotion but a selfless, sacrificial, patient, and kind commitment to the well-being of others. Jesus commanded His disciples, "A new commandment I give to you, that you love one another: just as I have loved you, you also are to love one another" (John 13:34). This Christ-like love, described so richly in 1 Corinthians 13, seeks the other's good, forgives readily, endures patiently, and hopes steadfastly. It is the soil in which all other relational virtues grow.

Mutual Submission and Service (Ephesians 5:21, Philippians 2:3-4): Humility is the air that healthy relationships breathe. The principle of mutual submission, "submitting to one another out of reverence for Christ" (Ephesians 5:21), calls believers to lay down their rights and preferences for the sake of others. Philippians 2:3-4 urges us to "Do nothing from selfish ambition or conceit, but in humility count others more significant than yourselves. Let each of you look not only to his own interests, but also to the interests of others." This mutual deference and servant-heartedness counteract the pride and self-centeredness that so often poison relationships.

Honesty and Truthfulness (Ephesians 4:15, 25): Authentic connection thrives in an atmosphere of truth. This means "speaking the truth in love" (Ephesians 4:15), being honest and transparent with one another, yet always with the aim of building up, not tearing down. Ephesians 4:25 commands, "Therefore, having put away falsehood, let each one of you speak the truth with his neighbor, for we are members one of another." This involves not only refraining from deceit but also courageously and compassionately addressing issues and speaking words that foster genuine understanding.

Forgiveness and Grace (Colossians 3:13, Ephesians 4:32): Given our fallen nature, no relationship will be free from offense or hurt. Therefore, forgiveness and grace are essential lubricants for maintaining healthy connections. We are called to be "bearing with one another and, if one has a complaint against another, forgiving each other; as the Lord has forgiven you, so you also must forgive" (Colossians 3:13). This mirrors the call in Ephesians 4:32 to be "kind to one another, tenderhearted, forgiving one another, as God in Christ forgave you." A willingness to extend grace and forgiveness, just as we have received it from God, is non-negotiable for lasting relationships.

Healthy Boundaries: While love calls us to openness and vulnerability, wisdom calls for healthy boundaries. Boundaries are not unloving walls designed to keep people out, but rather God-honoring limits that protect ourselves and our relationships from sin, harm, and disrespect. They define what is acceptable and unacceptable behavior within a relationship. The Bible implicitly supports boundaries through its warnings against associating with certain kinds of people (e.g., Proverbs on avoiding the quarrelsome or the easily angered) and its commands against participating in or enabling sin. Healthy boundaries are an expression of good stewardship over our lives and our relational well-being.

Effective Communication (James 1:19, Proverbs 15:1): Clear, respectful, and empathetic communication is vital. James 1:19 advises, "let every person be quick to hear, slow to speak, slow to anger." This involves active listening—seeking to understand before seeking to be understood—and thoughtful speech.

Proverbs 15:1 notes, "A soft answer turns away wrath, but a harsh word stirs up anger." Learning to communicate needs, feelings, and thoughts constructively, and to listen well to others, is a skill that undergirds all healthy interaction.

Bearing One Another's Burdens (Galatians 6:2): True community involves walking alongside each other in times of difficulty. "Bear one another's burdens, and so fulfill the law of Christ" (Galatians 6:2). This calls for empathy, practical support, and a willingness to share in the sorrows and struggles of our brothers and sisters in Christ. It is the opposite of a superficial or self-absorbed existence.

Encouragement and Edification (1 Thessalonians 5:11, Hebrews 10:24-25): Healthy relationships are characterized by mutual encouragement and a commitment to building one another up in the faith. "Therefore encourage one another and build one another up, just as you are doing" (1 Thessalonians 5:11). Hebrews 10:24-25 urges us to "consider how to stir up one another to love and good works, not neglecting to meet together, as is the habit of some, but encouraging one another." Our words and actions should aim to strengthen, comfort, and spur others on towards Christ-likeness.

These biblical principles provide a divine blueprint for relationships that not only heal but also sanctify, drawing us closer to God and to each other in ways that reflect the love and unity of the Trinity itself.

Building a Support Community

Understanding biblical principles for healthy relationships is foundational, but these principles are best lived out and experienced within the context of a supportive community. God has designed us for fellowship (*koinonia*); we are not meant to navigate the complexities of life or the journey of faith in isolation. Past pain can make the prospect of community daunting, potentially triggering fears of rejection or further hurt. However, intentionally building and participating in a healthy support community is a vital step in healing and in creating meaningful connections that reflect God's relational heart.

The Importance of Christian Fellowship (Koinonia): The New Testament paints a vivid picture of the early church as a community deeply intertwined in fellowship (Acts 2:42-47). This *koinonia* was characterized by shared life, mutual support, corporate worship, and a commitment to one another's spiritual and practical well-being. God designed the church to be a primary context where believers experience His love, grow in their faith, and find strength for life's journey. Isolation, conversely, can leave us vulnerable to discouragement, deception, and the perpetuation of unhealthy patterns.

Identifying Healthy Individuals and Communities: Not all communities or individuals are equally healthy or safe, especially for those recovering from past pain. Wisdom is needed in discerning where to invest relationally. Look for communities and individuals characterized by: * **Grace-filled atmosphere:** Where mistakes are met with understanding and forgiveness, not condemnation. * **Truth-speaking in love:** Where people are committed to biblical truth but communicate it with compassion and a desire for edification. * **Mutual support and encouragement:** Where members genuinely care for one another and actively seek to build each other up. * **Christ-centered focus:** Where the person and work of Jesus Christ are central to the community's life and mission. * **Respect for boundaries:** Where individual limits and needs are acknowledged and respected.

Taking Risks in Vulnerability (Wisely): Building deep connections requires vulnerability, which can be terrifying if past experiences have taught us that opening up leads to pain. However, vulnerability is the pathway to intimacy. The key is to take *wise* risks. This means starting small, perhaps with one or two individuals who have demonstrated trustworthiness and Christ-like character. Share a little at a time, gauging the response. Healthy individuals will respond with empathy and respect, creating a safer space for deeper sharing over time. It is not about baring your soul to everyone, but about discerningly choosing safe people with whom to be authentic.

Being a Good Friend/Community Member: Healthy relationships are reciprocal. As we seek support, we must also be willing to offer it. This involves practicing the biblical principles discussed earlier: loving sacrificially, serving humbly, speaking truth with grace, forgiving readily, listening actively, and encouraging consistently. Being a reliable, trustworthy, and supportive presence in the lives of others contributes to the overall health of the community and deepens our own connections.

The Local Church as Primary Community: For the Christian, the local church is intended by God to be the primary expression of supportive community. It is within a committed body of believers that we regularly gather for worship, receive biblical teaching, participate in the ordinances, and engage in mutual ministry. Actively participating in the life of a healthy local church, beyond just Sunday attendance, is crucial for building lasting, supportive relationships.

Small Groups, Mentors, Trusted Friends: Within the larger church community, smaller contexts often provide the best opportunities for deeper connection. Small groups focused on Bible study, prayer, and fellowship can foster intimacy and accountability. Seeking out a godly mentor, someone further along in their faith journey, can provide invaluable guidance and support. Cultivating a few deep friendships with trusted believers who can speak into your life and walk with you through challenges is a precious gift.

Overcoming Barriers to Community: Many factors can hinder our engagement in community: fear of judgment, past hurts from other Christians or churches, cynicism about the possibility of genuine connection, or even practical challenges like busyness. Acknowledging these barriers is the first step. Prayerfully addressing these fears and hurts, perhaps with the help of a pastor or counselor, and making a conscious commitment to step out in faith, even when it feels risky, is essential. God often meets us and heals us *within* the context of His people, imperfect as they may be.

Building a support community is an active, ongoing process. It requires intentionality, patience, and a willingness to both give and receive. But the rewards—the shared joy, mutual encouragement, and tangible experience of God's love through His people—are immeasurable and indispensable for a life of meaningful connection.

Exercise: Creating Meaningful Connections Worksheet

This worksheet is designed to help you reflect on your current relational patterns, identify areas for growth based on biblical principles, and take intentional steps towards building healthier, more meaningful connections.

1. Reflect on Your Relational Patterns: Consider the common relational patterns that can emerge from pain (Avoidance/Withdrawal, Anxious Attachment/Clinginess, Mistrust/Suspicion, People-Pleasing, Conflict-Driven/Controlling Behaviors, Difficulty with Vulnerability).

- Which of these patterns, if any, do you recognize in your own life? Be specific.

  _____

  _____

- How do these patterns affect your current relationships? (with family, friends, colleagues, God)

  _____

  _____

2. Identify Biblical Principles for Growth: Review the "Biblical Principles for Healthy Relationships" section (Love, Mutual Submission/Service, Honesty/Truthfulness, Forgiveness/Grace, Healthy Boundaries, Effective Communication, Bearing Burdens, Encouragement/Edification).

- Which one or two of these principles do you feel a particular need to cultivate in your life right now to counteract the unhealthy patterns you identified?

_____

_____

_____

- Why are these principles important for you at this time?

_____

_____

_____

3. Assess Your Current Support Community: Think about your current network of relationships (church, small group, friends, family, mentors).

- In what ways does your current community provide support and reflect healthy biblical principles?

_____

_____

- Are there areas where your community life is lacking or where you feel disconnected?

_____

_____

4. Brainstorm Steps to Build/Strengthen Connections: Based on your reflections, what are some practical steps you can take to build new healthy connections or strengthen existing ones?

- One step I can take to be more vulnerable (wisely) with a trusted person is:

_____

_____

- One way I can actively participate more in my local church or a small group is:

_____

_____

- One specific biblical principle I can focus on practicing in a key relationship this week is:

_____

_____

(e.g., practice active listening with my spouse, offer encouragement to a friend, choose to forgive a minor offense).

5. Prayer for Healthy Connections: Write a short prayer asking God for wisdom, courage, and grace to cultivate meaningful, Christ-centered connections in your life. Ask Him to heal past relational wounds and to guide you in being a good friend and community member.

_____

_____

_____

Remember, creating meaningful connections is a journey that unfolds over time, with God's help and in the context of His people. Be patient with yourself and others, and celebrate the small steps of growth along the way. You were made for connection, and God desires to see you thrive in relationships that honor Him and bless others.

ELEVEN

Discovering Purpose Beyond Pain

> *"And we know that for those who love God all things work together for good, for those who are called according to his purpose."*
>
> Romans 8:28 (ESV)

O ur journey through the landscapes of forgiveness, surrender, identity, and connection now brings us to a profound and often elusive quest: discovering purpose beyond pain. When suffering touches our lives, it can cast a long shadow, making it difficult to see any meaning or direction. The pain itself can feel all-consuming, leading to a sense of aimless- ness or a belief that our potential for a purposeful life has been irrevocably damaged. However, from a Reformed theological perspective, God is a God of purpose, and even in our deepest pain, He is at work, weaving a narrative that ultimately points to His glory and our good. This chapter will explore how pain can distort our sense of purpose, delve into the biblical foundations of true purpose formation, consider the challenging yet vital concept of finding meaning in suffering, and conclude with a practical exercise to help you uncover and embrace the purpose God has for you, not in spite of your pain, but sometimes, even through it.

Purpose Distortions from Pain

Pain has a disorienting effect. It can act like a dense fog, obscuring our view of the future and distorting our understanding of our own significance and potential. When suffering is intense or prolonged, it can lead to several common distortions in our perception of purpose, leaving us feeling adrift or defined solely by our afflictions.

One common distortion is the **belief that pain negates purpose.** We might think, "How can my life have any meaning when I am dealing with so much suffering?" or "My illness/loss/trauma has robbed me of any chance to fulfill my purpose." Pain can feel like a full stop at the end of a sentence, rather than a comma or even a challenging chapter in a larger, unfolding story. The sheer effort of managing pain can consume all our energy, leaving little room to even contemplate a purpose beyond survival.

Another distortion is the **internalization of a victim identity that eclipses a purposeful identity.** While acknowledging victimhood is important in the face of genuine harm, allowing it to become our primary identity can be paralyzing. If we see ourselves solely as victims of circumstance or of others' actions, we may feel powerless to pursue any purpose. The narrative becomes one of passive suffering rather than active engagement with God's calling, however that might look in our current situation.

Pain can also lead to a **narrowing of perceived purpose to solely overcoming the pain itself.** While healing and managing suffering are valid and important pursuits, if they become the *only* focus, we can miss the broader purposes God may have for us even amidst our struggles. Our purpose is always larger than our pain, even when our pain is a significant part of our current experience.

Sometimes, pain can foster a **cynical or nihilistic view of purpose.** If we have experienced profound disappointment, loss, or what feels like meaningless suffering, we might begin to question whether there is any real purpose to life at all, for ourselves or for anyone. This can lead to despair, apathy, or a bitter resignation that sees all striving for meaning as futile. The goodness and overarching plan of God can become obscured by the immediacy and intensity of our hurt.

Furthermore, past pain can lead to **fear-based decision-making that steers us away from our true calling.** If previous attempts to pursue a goal or step out in faith resulted in pain or failure, we might become overly cautious, avoiding any risk or new endeavor that could potentially lead to more suffering. This fear can effectively shut down our willingness to explore or embrace the unique purposes God has for us, leading to a life lived far smaller than intended.

Finally, for those who once had a clear sense of purpose that was derailed by pain or illness (e.g., a career cut short, a ministry ended), there can be a profound **sense of lost purpose and a struggle to redefine it.** It can be difficult to see that God's purpose for us is not always tied to a specific role or ability, and that He can unfold new and unexpected avenues of purpose even when old ones have closed.

Recognizing these distortions is the first step toward challenging them with biblical truth and rediscovering that God's purposes for us are resilient, multifaceted, and ultimately rooted in His unchanging character and calling, not in our fluctuating circumstances or pain levels.

Biblical Purpose Formation

In stark contrast to the distortions that pain can introduce, the Bible presents a robust and hope-filled understanding of purpose. From a Reformed theological standpoint, our ultimate purpose is rooted in the sovereign will and glory of God. It is not something we invent for ourselves but something we discover and align ourselves with as we come to know God and His work in the world. This biblical framework for purpose formation provides an anchor that can hold steady even amidst the storms of suffering.

The Chief End of Man: To Glorify God and Enjoy Him Forever. This statement from the Westminster Shorter Catechism encapsulates the foundational purpose of human existence. Our primary calling is not self-fulfillment in the worldly sense, but to live in such a way that our lives bring glory to God (1 Corinthians 10:31). This purpose is vast and all-encompassing, able to be pursued in every circumstance, whether in joy or sorrow, health or sickness. Enjoying God forever speaks to the deep, satisfying relationship we are created to have with Him, a relationship that itself is a core aspect of our purpose.

Purpose Rooted in Creation and Redemption. God created humanity in His image (Genesis 1:26-27) with inherent purpose: to reflect His character, to steward His creation, and to live in fellowship with Him. Though sin marred this original design, God's redemptive plan in Christ not only restores us to fellowship with Him but also renews and re-commissions us for His purposes. As new creations in Christ (2 Corinthians 5:17), we are "created in Christ Jesus for good works, which God prepared beforehand, that we should walk in them" (Ephesians 2:10). Our purpose, therefore, is not lost due to sin or suffering but is actually reframed and empowered through Christ's redemptive work.

God's Sovereignty and Our Purpose. A key tenet of Reformed theology is God's meticulous sovereignty over all things. This means that our lives, including our unique gifts, circumstances, and even our pain, are not random but are part of His overarching plan. Romans 8:28 reminds us, "And we know that for those who love God all things work together for good, for those who are called according to his purpose." This truth doesn't mean pain is good in itself, but that God, in His sovereignty, can weave even the darkest threads of our experiences into a tapestry that fulfills His good purposes. Our purpose is not contingent on ideal circumstances but can be discovered and lived out within the specific context God has ordained for us.

Diverse Callings within a Unified Purpose. While our ultimate purpose is to glorify God, this is expressed through diverse callings and vocations. God equips each believer with unique spiritual gifts (1 Corinthians 12, Romans 12, Ephesians 4) for the building up of the body of Christ and for service in the world. Our purpose may involve our roles in our families, our work, our church, and our communities. It includes using our talents, resources, and experiences to love God and love our neighbor. Pain does not necessarily negate these callings; it may reshape them or open up new avenues for service that we had not previously considered (e.g., ministering to others who are suffering).

Purpose as a Journey of Faith and Obedience. Discovering and living out our God-given purpose is not usually a one-time revelation but a journey of faith and obedience. It involves seeking God's will through prayer and His Word, being sensitive to the Holy Spirit's leading, and faithfully taking the next step of obedience, even when the full picture is unclear. Our purpose unfolds as we walk with God, trusting His guidance and His timing.

Eternal Significance. Biblical purpose is not limited to our earthly lifespan. What we do in Christ for God's glory has eternal significance. This perspective lifts our gaze beyond our immediate struggles and imbues even seemingly small acts of faithfulness with profound meaning. We are part of a story that is much larger than ourselves, a story that culminates in the new heavens and new earth where God's purposes will be fully realized.

Understanding these biblical principles helps to reorient our search for purpose away from self-defined ambitions or circumstantial ease, and towards a God-centered vision that is resilient, meaningful, and ultimately fulfilling, regardless of the pain we may encounter along the way.

Finding Meaning in Suffering

The question of meaning in suffering is one of the oldest and most profound human inquiries. When pain enters our lives, it often brings with it a sense of randomness or even cruelty, making it difficult to perceive any underlying purpose. While the Bible does not offer simplistic answers that neatly tie up every loose end of our suffering, it does provide a framework for finding meaning *in* and *through* suffering, particularly from a Reformed theological perspective that emphasizes God's sovereignty and redemptive purposes.

God's Sovereignty Over Suffering: A foundational truth is that God is sovereign over all things, including suffering (Lamentations 3:37-38; Job 42:2; Ephesians 1:11). This does not mean God is the author of evil or that He delights in our pain. Rather, it means that nothing, not even our deepest afflictions, occurs outside of His ultimate control and permission. This truth, while sometimes hard to grasp, can be a source of profound comfort. If God is sovereign, then our suffering is not meaningless chaos but is, in some way known to Him, part of His larger, perfect plan.

Suffering as a Means of Sanctification and Character Formation (Romans 5:3-5, James 1:2-4): Scripture teaches that God uses suffering to refine our character and deepen our faith. Paul writes, "Not only that, but we rejoice in our sufferings, knowing that suffering produces endurance, and endurance produces character, and character produces hope" (Romans 5:3-4). James echoes this: "Count it all joy, my brothers, when you meet trials of various kinds, for you know that the testing of your faith produces steadfastness. And let steadfastness have its full effect, that you may be perfect and complete, lacking in nothing" (James 1:2-4). From this perspective, suffering, though painful, can be a crucible in which God forges Christ-like virtues such as patience, perseverance, humility, and a deeper reliance on Him. Meaning can be found in this transformative process.

Drawing Us Closer to God (Psalm 73:25-26, 2 Corinthians 1:8-9): Often, it is in times of deep suffering that we experience God's presence and comfort most profoundly. When earthly comforts and strengths fail, we are driven to depend on God in ways we might not otherwise. The psalmist, after wrestling with the prosperity of the wicked and his own afflictions, declares, "Whom have I in heaven but you? And there is nothing on earth that I desire besides you. My flesh and my heart may fail, but God is the strength of my heart and my portion forever" (Psalm 73:25-26). Paul speaks of being "so utterly burdened beyond our strength that we despaired of life itself... But that was to make us rely not on ourselves but on God who raises the dead" (2 Corinthians 1:8-9). Finding deeper intimacy with God amidst pain is a profound meaning in itself.

Equipping Us to Comfort Others (2 Corinthians 1:3-7): Our own experiences of suffering, when met with God's comfort, uniquely equip us to minister to others who are going through similar trials. Paul writes that God "comforts us in all our affliction, so that we may be able to comfort those who are in any affliction, with the comfort with which we ourselves are comforted by God" (2 Corinthians 1:4). Our pain, redeemed and comforted by God, can become a wellspring of empathy and effective ministry to a hurting world. This gives our suffering a purpose beyond our own experience.

Revealing God's Power in Our Weakness (2 Corinthians 12:9-10): The apostle Paul learned that God's power is made perfect in weakness. When Paul pleaded for the removal of his "thorn in the flesh," the Lord responded, "My grace is sufficient for you, for my power is made perfect in weakness." Paul's conclusion was, "Therefore I will boast all the more gladly of my weaknesses, so that the power of Christ may rest upon me... For when I am weak, then I am strong" (2 Corinthians 12:9-10). Suffering can strip away our self-reliance and become a platform for God's strength and grace to be displayed in and through us. This brings glory to God, which is our ultimate purpose.

Conforming Us to the Image of Christ (Romans 8:29, Philippians 3:10): God's ultimate purpose for believers is to conform them to the image of His Son, Jesus Christ (Romans 8:29). Christ Himself was a "man of sorrows, and acquainted with grief" (Isaiah 53:3). Sharing in His sufferings, in some measure, can be part of this conforming process, allowing us to know Him more deeply, including "the fellowship of his sufferings" (Philippians 3:10). Our pain can draw us into a deeper identification with our suffering Savior, who understands our trials perfectly.

Awaiting Future Glory (Romans 8:18, 2 Corinthians 4:17): The Bible consistently points us towards a future hope where all suffering will cease, and God's glory will be fully revealed. Paul states, "For I consider that the sufferings of this present time are not worth comparing with the glory that is to be revealed to us" (Romans 8:18). And again, "For this light momentary affliction is preparing for us an eternal weight of glory beyond all comparison" (2 Corinthians 4:17). This eternal perspective does not negate the present reality of pain, but it frames it within a larger narrative of ultimate redemption and glory, giving us hope and endurance.

Finding meaning in suffering is not about finding easy answers or pretending the pain doesn't hurt. It is about trusting in a sovereign God who is at work even in our darkest moments, using our afflictions for His glory, our sanctification, and the good of others, all while pointing us to an eternal hope that far outweighs our present trials.

Exercise: Discovering Purpose Beyond Pain

This exercise is designed to help you prayerfully reflect on God's purpose for your life, especially in light of any pain or suffering you have experienced or are experiencing. The goal is to begin discerning how God might be at work and what steps you can take to align with His purposes. Approach this with an open heart, seeking the Holy Spirit's guidance.

1. Reflect on Purpose Distortions: Review the section "Purpose Distortions from Pain." Identify any distortions that resonate with your own experience. Honesty here is key.

- Which (if any) of the listed purpose distortions have you experienced or are currently experiencing? (e.g., pain negates purpose, victim identity, pain as sole focus, cynicism, fear-based decisions, lost purpose).

_____

_____

_____

- How have these distortions affected your outlook or actions?

_____

_____

_____

2. Meditate on Biblical Purpose Formation: Consider the core biblical principles of purpose: glorifying God and enjoying Him forever, being created for good works prepared by God, His sovereign plan that works all things for good for those who love Him, diverse callings, purpose as a journey, and eternal significance. * Which of these biblical truths about purpose do you find most comforting or challenging right now? Why?

_____

_____

3. Explore Meaning in Your Suffering (If Applicable): Reflect on the ways God might be working, or desire to work, in and through your pain (refer to "Finding Meaning in Suffering" section: sanctification, drawing closer to God, equipping to comfort others, revealing His power, conforming to Christ, pointing to future glory).

- Are there any glimpses, however small, of how God might be using or could use your suffering for a greater purpose?

_____

_____

This is often a difficult area. If you are struggling to see any meaning, simply acknowledge that to God and ask for His perspective.

4. Identify Your Gifts, Passions, and Opportunities: Regardless of your pain, God has uniquely gifted you. Consider:

- What are some of your God-given talents, skills, or spiritual gifts?

_____

_____

- What are you passionate about? What needs or causes stir your heart?

_____

_____

- What opportunities for service or contribution (however small they may seem) are currently available to you, even within your limitations?

_____

_____

5. Brainstorm Potential Areas of Purpose: Based on your gifts, passions, opportunities, and your understanding of biblical purpose, brainstorm some potential ways you could live out God's purpose in your current season. Don't censor yourself; just list ideas.

_____

_____

6. Choose One Small Step: From your brainstormed list, choose one small, actionable step you can take this week to move towards living more purposefully, aligned with God's calling.

- My small step is:

_____

_____

- How does this step connect to glorifying God or serving others?

_____

_____

7. Prayer for Purpose: Write a prayer asking God to reveal His purpose for you more clearly, to heal any distortions caused by pain, and to give you the strength and wisdom to walk in the good works He has prepared for you.

_____

_____

_____

_____

Discovering purpose beyond pain is a journey of faith, trust, and active engagement with God. It's about shifting our focus from what pain has taken to what God can still do. He is a God of redemption and restoration, and His purposes for you are good, even when the path is difficult.

TWELVE

Maintaining Your Freedom

"Stand firm therefore, and do not submit again to a yoke of slavery."

Galatians 5:1 (ESV)

Our journey together through the challenging, yet ultimately hope-filled, landscapes of pain, forgiveness, surrender, identity, connection, and purpose has brought us to this concluding chapter. We have explored the depths of how suffering can impact us and, more importantly, how God's grace and truth offer a path not just to healing, but to a transformed life. However, the freedom we have discussed—freedom from the bondage of bitterness, the tyranny of uncontrolled thoughts, the distortions of a pain-defined identity, the isolation of broken relationships, and the despair of purposelessness—is not a one-time achievement that, once attained, requires no further attention. Rather, maintaining this precious, hard-won freedom is an ongoing process, a continuous journey of faith, vigilance, and active engagement with the spiritual disciplines and practical strategies that sustain it. This final chapter is dedicated to equipping you for this lifelong endeavor. We will acknowledge the ongoing nature of healing, discuss how to identify and manage triggers, explore vital spiritual practices for sustained freedom, offer practical strategies for daily life, and encourage you to fully embrace a life of enduring freedom and purpose in Christ.

The Ongoing Nature of Healing

One of the most crucial understandings for maintaining freedom is that healing is rarely a linear progression culminating in a final, static state of "cured." More often, particularly when dealing with deep wounds or chronic conditions, healing is an ongoing journey with ebbs and flows, moments of significant progress, and times where old struggles may resurface. This is not a sign of failure but a reflection of our human frailty and the persistent nature of sin and brokenness in this fallen world. Embracing the ongoing nature of healing sets realistic expectations and prepares us for sustained effort.

It is vital to recognize that maintaining freedom requires **vigilance and proactive engagement.** Just as a garden, once beautifully cultivated, needs consistent tending to prevent weeds from overtaking it, so our spiritual and emotional well-being requires ongoing attention. This involves being watchful over our hearts and minds (Proverbs 4:23), regularly practicing the spiritual disciplines that keep us connected to God, and being proactive in applying the truths and strategies we have learned. Complacency can be a subtle enemy, allowing old patterns or new challenges to erode the freedom we have gained.

Furthermore, it is important to **acknowledge that setbacks can happen and are not definitive failures.** There may be days when you feel triggered, when old anxieties resurface, or when you stumble in an area where you thought you had gained victory. In these moments, it is easy to feel discouraged or to believe that all progress has been lost. However, a setback is not the end of the story. It is an opportunity to re-engage with God's grace, to revisit the tools and truths that have helped before, and to learn and grow even from the struggle. From a Reformed perspective, our ultimate security and standing with God are not based on our perfect performance but on Christ's finished work. This assurance allows us to face setbacks with honesty and a renewed determination to press on, knowing that His grace is sufficient (2 Corinthians 12:9).

The journey of healing and maintaining freedom is a marathon, not a sprint. It requires patience with ourselves, perseverance in the face of challenges, and a continual reliance on God's sustaining grace. Understanding this ongoing nature helps us to cultivate a mindset of resilience and a commitment to the long-term process of sanctification and growth in Christ.

Identifying and Managing Triggers

A crucial aspect of maintaining freedom is learning to identify and manage triggers—those specific situations, people, thoughts, emotions, or even sensory inputs that can provoke a return to old, unhelpful patterns of thinking, feeling, or behaving. Triggers are often linked to past pain or trauma, and encountering them can feel like being suddenly pulled back into the vortex of old struggles. Developing an awareness of your personal triggers and having strategies to manage them is a proactive way to safeguard your freedom.

Common Triggers can vary widely from person to person, but some general categories include:

- **Stressful Life Events:** Major life changes, financial pressures, job difficulties, or relational conflicts can act as significant triggers, weakening our coping mechanisms.
- **Difficult Relationships or Relational Dynamics:** Interacting with individuals who were part of past painful experiences, or encountering relational patterns that mimic those experiences, can be highly triggering.
- **Anniversaries of Traumatic Events or Losses:** Specific dates or times of the year associated with past trauma or loss can bring a resurgence of grief, anxiety, or other difficult emotions.
- **Sensory Inputs:** Certain sights, sounds, smells, tastes, or physical sensations that were associated with past trauma can unexpectedly trigger a strong emotional or physiological response.
- **Negative Thought Patterns:** Allowing negative self-talk, catastrophic thinking, or dwelling on past hurts to take root can trigger a downward spiral of emotion and behavior.
- **Physical States:** Fatigue, illness, or hunger can lower our resilience and make us more susceptible to triggers.
- **Specific Environments:** Places associated with past negative experiences can also act as powerful triggers.

Developing Coping Mechanisms: Once potential triggers are identified, the next step is to develop healthy coping mechanisms. This is not about avoiding all triggers, which is often impossible, but about learning to respond to them in ways that reinforce freedom rather than undermine it. Some effective coping mechanisms include:

- **Deep Breathing and Grounding Techniques:** When a trigger causes anxiety or a feeling of being overwhelmed, simple techniques like deep, slow breathing can calm the nervous system. Grounding techniques, such as focusing on your five senses to connect with the present moment (what can you see, hear, smell, touch, taste right now?), can also be very helpful.
- **Prayer and Scripture Meditation:** Immediately turning to God in prayer when triggered, casting your anxiety on Him (1 Peter 5:7), and recalling relevant scriptural truths and promises can re-center your mind and heart on His strength and presence.
- **Mindfulness of Thoughts and Emotions:** Paying attention to your thoughts and emotions when triggered, without judgment but with curiosity, can help you to recognize them as temporary states rather than ultimate realities. This creates space to choose a different response.
- **Seeking Support:** Reaching out to a trusted friend, mentor, pastor, or counselor when you feel triggered can provide invaluable support, perspective, and accountability.
- **Engaging in Healthy Distractions or Self-Soothing Activities:** Sometimes, temporarily shifting your focus to a healthy, enjoyable activity (like going for a walk,

listening to uplifting music, engaging in a hobby) can help to de-escalate the intensity of a triggered response.

- **Reviewing Past Victories and God's Faithfulness:** Reminding yourself of how God has helped you overcome similar challenges in the past can bolster your faith and confidence in His ability to help you again.
- **Creating a Relapse Prevention Plan:** For those dealing with significant past trauma or addictive patterns, a more formal relapse prevention plan can be extremely beneficial. This involves:

Specifically identifying your high-risk triggers.

- **Listing early warning signs** that indicate you might be heading towards an unhelpful response.
- **Developing a clear list of coping strategies** that you will implement when triggered or when warning signs appear.
- **Identifying specific people in your support system** you can contact.
- **Having a plan for what to do if you do stumble** (e.g., confessing to God and a trusted person, re-engaging with support, not giving up).

Identifying and managing triggers is an ongoing learning process. It requires self-awareness, honesty, and a willingness to proactively engage with God's help. By doing so, you can significantly reduce the power of past pain to dictate your present and future, thereby maintaining and even deepening the freedom you have found in Christ.

Spiritual Practices for Sustained Freedom

While identifying triggers and developing coping mechanisms are crucial practical steps, the bedrock of sustained freedom lies in a vibrant, ongoing relationship with God, nurtured through consistent spiritual practices. These disciplines are not legalistic requirements for earning God's favor, but rather God-given means of grace through which we connect with Him, receive His strength, and are progressively transformed into the image of Christ. They are essential for maintaining spiritual vitality and resilience against the challenges that seek to erode our freedom.

Prayer and Meditation: Consistent, heartfelt prayer is the lifeline of the Christian. It is our direct communication with our Heavenly Father, a place where we can pour out our hearts, confess our sins, express our gratitude, seek His wisdom, and intercede for others. Maintaining freedom requires a commitment to regular prayer, not just in times of crisis, but as a daily rhythm. This includes not only petitionary prayer but also adoration, confession, and thanksgiving. Meditation, particularly on Scripture, complements prayer. It involves thoughtfully pondering God's Word, allowing its truths to sink deep into our hearts and minds, shaping our perspectives and renewing our spirits (Psalm 1:2, Joshua 1:8).

Scripture Reading and Study: The Bible is God's inspired and authoritative Word, our primary source for knowing Him, understanding His will, and finding guidance for life (2 Timothy 3:16-17). Regular engagement with Scripture—reading it, studying it, memorizing it, and applying it—is indispensable for sustained freedom. God's Word illuminates truth, exposes lies, corrects our thinking, encourages our hearts, and equips us for every good work. It is the sword of the Spirit (Ephesians 6:17) that helps us combat temptation and stand firm in our faith. A daily diet of

Scripture nourishes the soul and strengthens us against the deceptions that can lead us away from freedom.

Fellowship and Community: As explored in Chapter 10, God designed us for community. Sustained freedom is rarely maintained in isolation. Active participation in a healthy Christian fellowship provides mutual support, accountability, encouragement, and opportunities to both give and receive ministry (Hebrews 10:24-25). Being part of a local church, engaging in small groups, and cultivating deep, godly friendships create a web of relationships that can uphold us in times of weakness and celebrate with us in times of strength. Honest sharing within a trusted community can also provide perspective and correction when we are straying or struggling.

Worship and Gratitude: Corporate and private worship, focused on adoring God for who He is and what He has done, lifts our gaze from our problems to His majesty and power. Worship reorients our hearts and minds, reminding us of His sovereignty, love, and faithfulness. Closely allied with worship is the cultivation of gratitude. Intentionally thanking God for His blessings, both big and small, even amidst difficulties, shifts our perspective from what we lack to the abundance of His grace (1 Thessalonians 5:18). A grateful heart is more resilient and less susceptible to discontentment and bitterness, which can undermine freedom.

Serving Others: Shifting our focus from ourselves to the needs of others is a powerful antidote to self-absorption and a vital way to live out our God-given purpose. Jesus Himself came not to be served, but to serve (Mark 10:45). When we use our gifts and resources to serve others in love, we not only bless them but also experience a deeper sense of meaning and joy. Serving others can help maintain perspective on our own struggles and reinforce our identity as beloved children of God called to make a difference in the world. It is an active expression of our freedom in Christ, used for the good of His kingdom.

Regular Confession and Repentance: Since we continue to struggle with sin even as believers, regular confession and repentance are essential for maintaining a clear conscience and an unhindered relationship with God (1 John 1:9). When we stumble, promptly acknowledging our sin before God, seeking His forgiveness, and turning away from that sin (repentance) restores fellowship and prevents small compromises from growing into larger strongholds that threaten our freedom.

These spiritual practices are not a checklist for spiritual superiority but vital channels through which God's grace flows into our lives, empowering us to stand firm, grow in Christ, and maintain the freedom He has so graciously provided. They require intentionality and discipline, but the fruit they yield—a deeper relationship with God and sustained spiritual vitality—is immeasurable.

Practical Strategies for Daily Life

Alongside consistent spiritual practices, incorporating practical strategies into our daily lives can significantly bolster our efforts to maintain freedom. These strategies are about creating a lifestyle that supports well-being, resilience, and continued growth. They often involve intentional choices about how we manage our time, care for our bodies, engage our minds, and structure our environment to foster health rather than hinder it.

Establishing Healthy Routines: Our bodies and minds thrive on a degree of predictability and order. Establishing healthy routines for key areas of life can reduce stress and create a stable foundation for well-being.

Sleep: Prioritizing adequate, restful sleep is crucial. Sleep deprivation can significantly impact mood, cognitive function, and resilience, making us more vulnerable to triggers and negative thought patterns.

Nutrition: A balanced and nourishing diet provides the physical energy and mental clarity needed to navigate daily challenges. Conversely, poor nutrition can exacerbate stress and negatively affect mood.

Exercise: Regular physical activity is a powerful tool for managing stress, improving mood (through the release of endorphins), and boosting overall health. Finding an enjoyable form of exercise and incorporating it regularly into your routine can make a significant difference.

Spiritual Disciplines: As discussed previously, building spiritual practices like prayer and Scripture reading into a daily routine ensures they don't get crowded out by the demands of life.

Setting and Maintaining Healthy Boundaries: We touched on boundaries in the context of relationships (Chapter 10), but they are also vital for managing our time, energy, and commitments. Learning to say "no" to things that overextend us or pull us away from our core priorities is essential for preventing burnout and maintaining emotional and spiritual health. This includes boundaries with work, social engagements, and even media consumption. Protecting your time and energy allows you to invest them in ways that align with your values and support your freedom.

Mindfulness and Self-Awareness: Cultivating mindfulness—paying attention to the present moment without judgment—can be a powerful tool for maintaining freedom. This involves becoming more aware of your thoughts, emotions, and bodily sensations as they arise. Such self-awareness allows you to recognize early warning signs of stress, negative thinking, or emotional reactivity, giving you an opportunity to intervene constructively before these patterns take hold. It is about observing your inner state with a compassionate and curious stance, which can create space for more intentional responses rather than habitual reactions.

Continued Learning and Growth: A commitment to lifelong learning and personal growth is another key strategy. This might involve reading books (like this one!), attending workshops or seminars, listening to edifying podcasts, or even pursuing further education or counseling if needed. The journey of healing and sanctification is ongoing, and there is always more to learn about God, ourselves, and how to live wisely and fruitfully. A teachable spirit and a desire to grow keep us moving forward.

Creating a Supportive Environment: Our physical environment can also impact our well-being. To the extent possible, creating a home and work environment that is peaceful, orderly, and conducive to health can reduce stress and support our efforts to maintain freedom. This might involve decluttering, organizing, or personalizing your space in ways that promote calm and focus.

Practicing Gratitude Deliberately: Beyond the spiritual discipline of thanking God, actively practicing gratitude in daily life—perhaps by keeping a gratitude journal or regularly expressing appreciation to others—can rewire our brains to focus more on the positive and less on the negative. This fosters contentment and resilience.

Seeking Professional Help When Needed: There is no shame in recognizing when professional help from a Christian counselor, therapist, or psychologist is needed. Sometimes, the depth of past trauma, the complexity of mental health challenges, or the persistence of destructive patterns requires the specialized skills and support of a trained professional. Seeking such help is a sign of wisdom and strength, not weakness, and can be a vital component of maintaining long-term freedom and well-being.

These practical strategies, when integrated into daily life, work synergistically with spiritual practices to create a robust framework for maintaining the freedom found in Christ. They are about stewarding all aspects of our lives—body, mind, and spirit—in a way that honors God and promotes lasting health.

Embracing a Life of Freedom and Purpose

As we conclude this journey from pain to purpose, the ultimate invitation is to fully embrace the life of freedom and purpose that God offers in Jesus Christ. This is not a life free from all difficulty or struggle, for we still live in a fallen world. However, it is a life increasingly characterized by the fruit of the Spirit—love, joy, peace, patience, kindness, goodness, faithfulness, gentleness, and self-control (Galatians 5:22-23)—even amidst challenges. It is a life lived with a deep sense of meaning, rooted in God's eternal purposes and expressed through loving Him and loving others.

Embracing this life involves a **conscious and ongoing choice.** It is choosing daily to walk in the truth of who you are in Christ, to apply the principles of forgiveness and surrender, to cultivate healthy connections, and to live out your God-given purpose. It means choosing to rely on God's grace rather than your own strength, and to get back up with His help when you stumble.

It also involves **living with an eternal perspective.** The freedoms we experience now are a foretaste of the ultimate freedom and wholeness that await us in glory. Keeping our eyes fixed on Jesus, the author and perfecter of our faith (Hebrews 12:2), and on the hope of eternity, provides profound motivation and endurance for the journey. This perspective helps us to hold loosely to the things of this world and to invest in what has eternal value.

Furthermore, embracing a life of freedom and purpose means becoming a **conduit of God's grace and hope to others.** As you have received comfort and healing from God, you are uniquely positioned to share that comfort and hope with a hurting world. Your story, with all its pain and all its redemption, becomes a powerful testimony to God's faithfulness. Living purposefully often involves looking beyond ourselves to see how God can use us to bless and serve others, extending the freedom we have found.

Finally, embrace this life with **joy and gratitude.** The journey from pain to purpose, while arduous at times, is ultimately a journey into the abundant life that Jesus promised (John 10:10). Rejoice in the progress you have made, be thankful for God's unwavering love and grace, and look forward with anticipation to all that He still has in store for you. Your pain does not have the final say. God's redemptive purpose does.

May you go forth from reading this book not just with new knowledge, but with a renewed spirit, practical tools, and a deeper commitment to maintaining the precious freedom that is yours in Christ, living each day with purpose, for His glory.

Exercise: Maintaining Your Freedom Action Plan

This final worksheet is designed to help you synthesize what you have learned throughout this book and create a personalized action plan for maintaining your freedom and continuing to live a life of purpose in Christ. This is a plan to revisit and revise as you continue your journey.

1. Key Learnings and Takeaways: Reflect on the entire book. What are two or three of the most significant insights, principles, or truths that have impacted you?

Insight/Principle 1: _____

Why was this significant for you? _____

Insight/Principle 2: _____

Why was this significant for you? _____

Insight/Principle 3: _____

Why was this significant for you? _____

2. Identifying Ongoing Challenges/Vulnerabilities: Honestly assess areas where you still feel vulnerable or anticipate ongoing challenges to maintaining your freedom (e.g., specific triggers, thought patterns, relational dynamics, spiritual disciplines you struggle with).

Challenge/Vulnerability 1: _____

Challenge/Vulnerability 2: _____

Challenge/Vulnerability 3: _____

3. Core Spiritual Practices for Your Sustenance: From the spiritual practices discussed (Prayer/Meditation, Scripture, Fellowship, Worship/Gratitude, Service, Confession/Repentance), which 2-3 will you prioritize as foundational for your ongoing freedom and growth? How will you practically incorporate them into your life?

Practice 1: _____ Practical Step: _____

Practice 2: _____ Practical Step: _____

Practice 3: _____ Practical Step: _____

4. Key Practical Strategies for Your Lifestyle: From the practical strategies discussed (Healthy Routines, Boundaries, Mindfulness/Self-Awareness, Continued Learning, Supportive Environment, Gratitude, Professional Help), which 2-3 will you focus on implementing or strengthening?

Strategy 1: _____ Practical Step: _____

Strategy 2: _____ Practical Step: _____

Strategy 3: _____ Practical Step: _____

5. Your Support System: Identify key people in your life who can support you in maintaining your freedom. (e.g., spouse, trusted friend, mentor, pastor, small group, counselor)

_____

_____

How can you proactively engage with your support system?

_____

_____

6. A Commitment Statement for Embracing Freedom and Purpose: Write a brief personal commitment statement to God, affirming your desire to maintain the freedom He has given you and to live purposefully for His glory. This is for your own encouragement and resolve.

_____

_____

_____

7. Next Steps and Long-Term Vision: What is one immediate next step you will take based on this action plan?

_____

_____

Looking ahead, what is your vision for a life lived in sustained freedom and purpose, five years from now? (Dream a little, rooted in God's promises.)

_____

_____

May God bless you richly as you continue to walk in the light of His truth and the power of His Spirit, maintaining your freedom and living out the beautiful purpose He has for your life.

Closing Thoughts: The Unfolding Journey

As we draw this exploration of "Untethered: The Journey from Pain to Purpose" to a close, it is my sincere hope that the words within these pages have served as a faithful companion, a source of comfort, and a guide towards the enduring freedom and profound purpose that can be found in Jesus Christ, even amidst the deepest valleys of suffering. The journey we have traversed together—from understanding the narratives that bind us, to embracing forgiveness and surrender, to rebuilding our identity in Christ, fostering meaningful connections, discovering purpose beyond our pain, and finally, to maintaining that hard-won freedom—is not a linear path with a definitive endpoint, but rather an ongoing, unfolding pilgrimage of faith.

Life in this fallen world will inevitably present us with challenges, and the echoes of past pain may at times resurface. Yet, the truth of God's unwavering love, His sovereign grace, and His redemptive power remains our constant anchor. The principles and practices discussed are not meant to be a one-time fix, but rather tools to be revisited, refined, and reapplied as we continue to grow in our walk with the Lord. The journey of sanctification is lifelong, and each step, even those that feel like a struggle, is an opportunity to lean more fully into His strength and to witness His faithfulness anew.

Remember that you are not alone on this path. The God who began a good work in you will carry it on to completion until the day of Christ Jesus (Philippians 1:6). He is with you, He is for you, and His Spirit empowers you. The community of faith, the body of Christ, is also there to walk alongside you, offering support, encouragement, and fellowship.

May the truths explored in this book take deep root in your heart, transforming not just your understanding, but the very way you live, love, and serve. May you continue to untether yourself from the things that would hold you back from the abundant life Christ offers—the bitterness of unforgiveness, the burden of self-reliance, the distortions of a pain-defined identity, the isolation of fear, and the despair of meaninglessness.

Instead, may you be increasingly tethered to Him: to His Word, His love, His purposes, and His unfailing grace. May your life become a testament to His redemptive power, a story of how He takes our broken pieces and creates something beautiful for His glory. The journey from pain to purpose is indeed profound, and it is a journey He invites each of us to walk with Him, day by day, until we see Him face to face.

Thank You for Reading, and Blessings

Thank you for taking the time to journey through these pages. It is my prayer that the reflections and exercises within "Untethered" have been a source of encouragement, insight, and practical help as you navigate your own path from pain to purpose.

May the Lord bless you and keep you; may He make His face shine upon you and be gracious to you; may He lift up His countenance upon you and give you peace, now and always.

Blessings,

   - Rudolph Visser

Bibliography

On Christian Suffering

Alcorn, Randy. *If God Is Good: Faith in the Midst of Suffering and Evil*. Colorado Springs, CO: Multnomah, 2009.

Boston, Thomas. *The Crook in the Lot*. Edinburgh: Banner of Truth, 2010.

Keller, Timothy. *Walking with God Through Pain and Suffering*. New York: Dutton, 2013.

Lewis, C. S. *The Problem of Pain*. New York: HarperOne, 2001.

Peterman, Gerald W., and Andrew J. Schmutzer. *Between Pain and Grace: A Biblical Theology of Suffering*. Chicago: Moody Publishers, 2016.

Piper, John, and Justin Taylor, eds. *Suffering and the Sovereignty of God*. Wheaton, IL: Crossway, 2006.

Rutherford, Samuel. *The Loveliness of Christ*. Edinburgh: Banner of Truth, 2007.

Sproul, R. C. *Surprised by Suffering: The Role of Pain and Death in the Christian Life*. Sanford, FL: Reformation Trust, 2009.

Tada, Joni Eareckson. *Joni: An Unforgettable Story*. Grand Rapids, MI: Zondervan, 1976.

Welch, Edward T. *When I Am Afraid: A Step-by-Step Guide Away from Fear and Anxiety*. Greensboro, NC: New Growth Press, 2008.

On Finding Purpose (Christian Perspective)

Buechner, Frederick. *Wishful Thinking: A Theological ABC*. San Francisco: Harper & Row, 1973.

Eldredge, John. *Wild at Heart: Discovering the Secret of a Man's Soul*. Nashville, TN: Thomas Nelson, 2001.

Frankl, Viktor E. *Man's Search for Meaning*. Boston: Beacon Press, 1959.

Guinness, Os. *The Call: Finding and Fulfilling the Central Purpose of Your Life*. Nashville, TN: Word Publishing, 1998.

MacDonald, Gordon. *Ordering Your Private World*. Nashville, TN: Oliver Nelson, 1984.

Palmer, Parker J. *Let Your Life Speak: Listening for the Voice of Vocation*. San Francisco: Jossey-Bass, 2000.

Peterson, Eugene H. *A Long Obedience in the Same Direction: Discipleship in an Instant Society*. Downers Grove, IL: InterVarsity Press, 1980.

Stott, John R. W. *Your Mind Matters: The Place of the Mind in the Christian Life*. Downers Grove, IL: InterVarsity Press, 1972.

Willard, Dallas. *The Divine Conspiracy: Rediscovering Our Hidden Life In God*. San Francisco: HarperSanFrancisco, 1998.

DeYoung, Kevin. *Just Do Something: A Liberating Approach to Finding God's Will*. Chicago: Moody Publishers, 2009.

On Healing from Pain (Christian Perspective)

Allender, Dan B. *The Wounded Heart: Hope for Adult Victims of Childhood Sexual Abuse*. Colorado Springs, CO: NavPress, 1990.

Backus, William. *The Healing Power of a Christian Mind*. Minneapolis, MN: Bethany House Publishers, 1985.

Crabb, Larry. *Inside Out*. Colorado Springs, CO: NavPress, 1988.

Lusko, Levi. *Through the Eyes of a Lion: Facing Impossible Pain, Finding Incredible Power*. Nashville, TN: Thomas Nelson, 2015.

Seamands, David A. *Healing for Damaged Emotions*. Colorado Springs, CO: Victor Books, 1981.

Smedes, Lewis B. *Forgive and Forget: Healing the Hurts We Don't Deserve*. San Francisco: HarperSanFrancisco, 1984.

Tracy, Steven R. *Mending the Soul: Understanding and Healing Abuse*. Grand Rapids, MI: Zondervan, 2005.

Welch, Edward T. *Shame Interrupted: How God Lifts the Pain of Worthlessness and Rejection*. Greensboro, NC: New Growth Press, 2012.

Welch, Edward T. *When People Are Big and God Is Small*. Phillipsburg, NJ: P&R Publishing, 1997.

Powlison, David. *Speaking Truth in Love: Counsel in Community*. Greensboro, NC: New Growth Press, 2005.

On Reformed Theology

Beeke, Joel R., and Mark Jones. *A Puritan Theology: Doctrine for Life*. Grand Rapids, MI: Reformation Heritage Books, 2012.

Berkhof, Louis. *Systematic Theology*. Grand Rapids, MI: Eerdmans, 1938.

Calvin, John. *Institutes of the Christian Religion*. Translated by Henry Beveridge. Edinburgh: Calvin Translation Society, 1845.

Grudem, Wayne. *Systematic Theology: An Introduction to Biblical Doctrine*. Grand Rapids, MI: Zondervan, 1994.

Hodge, Charles. *Systematic Theology*. 3 vols. New York: Charles Scribner & Co., 1871–1873.

Packer, J. I. *Knowing God*. Downers Grove, IL: InterVarsity Press, 1973.

Piper, John. *Desiring God: Meditations of a Christian Hedonist*. Sisters, OR: Multnomah Books, 1986.

Sproul, R. C. *The Holiness of God*. Wheaton, IL: Tyndale House Publishers, 1985.

Vos, Geerhardus. *Biblical Theology: Old and New Testaments*. Grand Rapids, MI: Eerdmans, 1948.

Warfield, B. B. *The Inspiration and Authority of the Bible*. Edited by Samuel G. Craig. Phillipsburg, NJ: Presbyterian and Reformed Publishing, 1948.

More Contemporary Resources

Earley, Dave, and Rod Dempsey. *Disciple Making Is...: How to Live the Great Commission with Passion and Confidence*. Nashville, TN: B&H Academic, 2013.

Fitzpatrick, Elyse M., and Dennis E. Johnson. *Counsel from the Cross: Connecting Broken People to the Love of Christ*. Wheaton, IL: Crossway, 2009.

Groeschel, Craig. *Winning the War in Your Mind: Change Your Thinking, Change Your Life*. Grand Rapids, MI: Zondervan, 2021.

Hunter, James Davison. *To Change the World: The Irony, Tragedy, and Possibility of Christianity in the Late Modern World*. New York: Oxford University Press, 2010.

Ingram, Chip. *The Real God: How He Longs for You to See Him*. Grand Rapids, MI: Baker Books, 2016.

Johnson, Jeff. *Got Purpose? God's Vision for Your Life*. Sisters, OR: Deep River Books, 2022.

Martin, Jonathan. *How to Survive a Shipwreck: Help Is on the Way and Love Is Already Here*. Grand Rapids, MI: Zondervan, 2016.

Nieuwhof, Carey. *Didn't See It Coming: Overcoming the Seven Greatest Challenges That No One Expects and Everyone Experiences*. Colorado Springs, CO: WaterBrook, 2018.

Ortberg, John. *Soul Keeping: Caring for the Most Important Part of You*. Grand Rapids, MI: Zondervan, 2014.

Reeder, Harry L. III. *From Embers to a Flame: How God Can Revitalize Your Church*. Phillipsburg, NJ: P&R Publishing, 2008.

Sauls, Scott. *Jesus Outside the Lines: A Way Forward for Those Who Are Tired of Taking Sides*. Carol Stream, IL: Tyndale House Publishers, 2015.

Scazzero, Peter. *Emotionally Healthy Spirituality: It's Impossible to Be Spiritually Mature, While Remaining Emotionally Immature*. Grand Rapids, MI: Zondervan, 2017.

Smith, James K. A. *You Are What You Love: The Spiritual Power of Habit.* Grand Rapids, MI: Brazos Press, 2016.

Stanley, Andy. *Better Decisions, Fewer Regrets: 5 Questions to Help You Determine Your Next Move.* Grand Rapids, MI: Zondervan, 2020.

Tripp, Paul David. *Instruments in the Redeemer's Hands: People in Need of Change Helping People in Need of Change.* Phillipsburg, NJ: P&R Publishing, 2002.